The Business Owner's Guide to
Reading and Understanding Financial Statements

The Business Owner's Guide to
Reading and Understanding Financial Statements

How to Budget, Forecast, and Monitor Cash Flow for Better Decision Making

Lita Epstein, MBA

WILEY

John Wiley & Sons, Inc.

Published by John Wiley & Sons, Inc., Hoboken, New Jersey.
Published simultaneously in Canada.

No part of this publication may be reproduced, stored in a retrieval system, or transmitted in any form or by any means, electronic, mechanical, photocopying, recording, scanning, or otherwise, except as permitted under Section 107 or 108 of the 1976 United States Copyright Act, without either the prior written permission of the Publisher, or authorization through payment of the appropriate per-copy fee to the Copyright Clearance Center, Inc., 222 Rosewood Drive, Danvers, MA 01923, (978) 750-8400, fax (978) 646-8600, or on the web at www.copyright.com. Requests to the Publisher for permission should be addressed to the Permissions Department, John Wiley & Sons, Inc., 111 River Street, Hoboken, NJ 07030, (201) 748-6011, fax (201) 748-6008, or online at http://www.wiley.com/go/permissions.

Limit of Liability/Disclaimer of Warranty: While the publisher and author have used their best efforts in preparing this book, they make no representations or warranties with respect to the accuracy or completeness of the contents of this book and specifically disclaim any implied warranties of merchantability or fitness for a particular purpose. No warranty may be created or extended by sales representatives or written sales materials. The advice and strategies contained herein may not be suitable for your situation. You should consult with a professional where appropriate. Neither the publisher nor author shall be liable for any loss of profit or any other commercial damages, including but not limited to special, incidental, consequential, or other damages.

For general information on our other products and services or for technical support, please contact our Customer Care Department within the United States at (800) 762-2974, outside the United States at (317) 572-3993 or fax (317) 572-4002.

Wiley publishes in a variety of print and electronic formats and by print-on-demand. Some material included with standard print versions of this book may not be included in e-books or in print-on-demand. If this book refers to media such as a CD or DVD that is not included in the version you purchased, you may download this material at http://booksupport.wiley.com. For more information about Wiley products, visit www.wiley.com.

Library of Congress Cataloging-in-Publication Data:

Epstein, Lita.
    The business owner's guide to reading and understanding financial statements : how to budget, forecast, and monitor cash flow for better decision making / Lita Epstein.
        p. cm.
    Includes index.
    ISBN 978-1-118-14351-3 (paper); ISBN 978-1-118-22558-5 (ebk);
    ISBN 978-1-118-23109-8 (ebk); ISBN 978-1-118-23112-8 (ebk)
        1. Cash flow.   2. Decision making.   3. Financial statements.
        4. Corporations—Finance.   I. Title.
    HF5681.C28E67   2012
    658.15'12—dc23

                                                                    2011038806

Printed in the United States of America
10 9 8 7 6 5 4 3 2 1

To my father,
Jerome Kirschbrown,
an auditor and a savings-and-loan examiner,
who helped me hone my financial skills
and taught me to use those skills
to improve a business's bottom line.

Contents

CONTENTS

Preface

Most small-business owners become very familiar with the income statement, which you may also know as the profit and loss statement, statement of operations, statement of earnings, or statement of operating results. Whatever you call it, this statement gives you a summary of the financial results of your business's operations over a certain period of time.

The bottom line of the income statement can be a net profit or a net loss. As long as the bottom line shows a profit and the overall trend is upward, many business owners are happy to receive this detail from their accountant and then go back to running their business.

Are business owners doing enough? With the U.S. Small Business Administration concluding that the five-year survival rate for new businesses is just over 50 percent, clearly this information combined with a business owner's experience is not enough for about half of all new business owners.

Why do businesses fail? Among the top 10 answers are five that can be directly tied to the need for better understanding of financial statements:

1. Insufficient cash
2. Poor inventory management
3. Overinvestment in fixed assets

4. Poor credit arrangements

5. Unexpected growth

The income statement alone cannot help you deal with any of these five problems. You need to have a better working knowledge of what goes into the income statement as well as two other key financial statements—the balance sheet and the statement of cash flows—to really get a handle on whether your business will succeed or fail.

LOOK BEHIND THE NUMBERS

Few business owners take a closer look behind the numbers that are collected to produce an income statement. Nor do they pay much attention to the numbers behind the other two key external reports: the balance sheet and the statement of cash flows. Even fewer develop customized internal financial statements to keep on top of their business's financial health.

These internal statements don't require extra data collection—the data are already being collected to prepare the three main external financial reports. By designing internal financial reports, you can use data already being collected to get a more complete picture of what's happening in your business.

In this book, I help you get a better understanding of the data collected to develop the key external financial statements. I give you some tools for developing internal financial statements so that you'll have a better handle on your business's financial health by taking a closer look at such things as your customer's payment habits, your inventory turnover, and your cost control.

First, let's take a quick look at the balance sheet and statement of cash flows. The balance sheet gives you a snapshot of how much you own, how much you owe, and how much equity you have in your business as of a particular date. I delve more deeply into how you can use the statement to measure your financial results in Chapter 2, "Balancing the Books: Your Assets and Liabilities."

The statement of cash flows does just that; it reviews what cash has come into the business and what cash has gone out. The bottom line of this statement is your net cash position, which can be very different from your net profit. I help you understand why that's the case as we delve further into this topic in Chapter 4, "Cash Is King."

With the knowledge you'll gain from having a better understanding of how to use the financial statements, you can analyze how well your business is doing and make course corrections quickly to keep your business profitable. In this book, I take you through a crash course on what data go into each of the three key financial statements and how you can use these statements to gauge the profitability of your company, get a handle on your company's liquidity, and test your company's cash position.

CUSTOMIZE YOUR INTERNAL REPORTING

Once you've completed this crash course on how to make the best use of these financial statements—which include the external reports that you must provide to your bankers, vendors, government entities, and others with whom you do business that require financial reporting—I take a closer look at internal reports you can develop to keep even better tabs on your company's financial well-being.

Internal reports are the kinds of reports that include detail you don't want outsiders to see. For example, if you sell your product by providing credit to your customers, you need to monitor whether your customers are paying you on time. If they aren't, your cash flow will be negatively impacted and your business's ability to continue to operate could be at risk. Even though your income statement is showing a profit because of the revenue earned, your company could be heading to a cash flow disaster.

Of course, you don't want outsiders to know the details of even who your customers are, so instead you develop an internal report called an Accounts Receivable Aging Schedule. This report details who's paying on time and who's late—and how late they are. You need to decide when you want to cut off a customer who's past due. In Chapter 7, "Monitoring Customer Collections," I give you the tools you need to help you determine this and other questions you may have about collecting the money due on time using internal reporting and analysis.

Another key area in which internal reports can help you improve your bottom line is gauging your success in moving your inventory, which I take a closer look at in Chapter 6, "Managing Inventory." In addition to moving that inventory—especially if you are operating a manufacturing business—you need to monitor its costs, which I discuss in Chapter 9, "Getting a Handle on Costs." Using internal reports, you can track cost trends and adjust pricing before it has a negative impact on your bottom line.

You've probably used discounts and special pricing to entice customers (or buyers for major stores) to buy your products, but do you know how much impact those discounts have on your bottom line? In Chapter 8, "Discounts and Special Pricing," I show you how to use internal reporting to track those impacts so you can adjust your month-end and year-end projections to account for that impact. Making use of discounts and special pricing without monitoring their impact on your overall profitability could lead to a business disaster of insufficient cash and disappointing profit results.

In Chapter 10, "Reducing Payouts," I take a closer look at proper bill pay management and how that can help you reduce your cash outlay. I discuss some simple steps you can take to be sure your bookkeeping staff is taking advantage of all vendor discounts by paying within a certain period of time, which can improve your bottom line.

Internal reports can help you make these key decisions:

- Determining which of your company's products produce a profit and which produce a loss.

- Determining what parts of the company should receive additional resources to encourage growth.

- Identifying unsuccessful parts of your business and making needed changes to turn the troubled project around or kill the project.

- Determining appropriate staffing and inventory levels that you need to meet customer demand.

There is no limit to the variety of internal reports you can create to manage your company effectively. There are no accounting rules one must follow when designing internal statements. In this book I give you some tools to get you started, but working with your accountants and your managers you can design reports that help you make decisions about key issues that impact your business's success using data already collected for the external reports.

BUDGETING FOR RESULTS

All these internal reports will be based on proper budgeting, which I talk about in Chapter 5, "Why Budgeting Is Important." You may or may not operate using a well-thought-out budget. Many business owners prepare a budget as part of their business plan and then ignore it most of the year. At the end of the year, they take a look to see how well they guessed at the results.

That's not necessarily a smart way of doing things. Budgeting on a month-by-month or even week-by-week basis can help you keep an eye on how well your business is doing. By developing a realistic budget up front and then monitoring your success at staying on budget, you can quickly recognize red flags that could lead to disaster year-end if changes aren't made. I show you how to use internal reports to help you quickly find those red flags so you can make a change midstream.

For example, you could have developed your anticipated revenues based on a certain level of sales, but because of an economic downturn you have no chance of reaching that level. If you quickly adjust the rest of your budget to reflect reality, you can probably avoid a major cash flow problem. It could mean reducing staff to reflect the slower pace of business, as well as reducing product orders. If you own a manufacturing company, it could mean you should reduce production.

Just as dangerous, the opposite could happen after you developed your budget for the year. The economy could recover more quickly than you anticipated, and you won't have enough products to meet sales demand unless you adjust your budget projections and order or produce more products. Maybe you'll even need to hire more staff than you had planned to meet demand. If you don't have the product available or the staff you need, you could lose customers to your competitors.

Developing realistic budgets and then using them to monitor your business can help you stay alive in both good times and bad. They enable you to make corrections midyear so that you don't face a period of insufficient cash, poor inventory management, not enough credit (or paying too much for credit), and unexpected growth.

Yes, unexpected growth can be just as devastating to a new business as a reduction in business. A new business that can't meet its demands from customers is more likely to lose them because the new business owner may not be able to depend on long-term customer loyalty. Whereas a well-established business may be able to hold on to its loyal customers if a product the customer wants is not immediately available, a new business won't likely have had time to build that customer loyalty. Instead, the new business owner will likely lose the sale to a competitor.

So let's get started on this journey to delve into financial statements and how they can improve your business's chance of success. I start in Chapter 1 by looking at the role the three key financial statements play in tracking your business's results.

Acknowledgments

I would like to thank all the people at John Wiley & Sons, Inc. who helped make this book possible, especially my acquisitions editor, Lauren Murphy, who first approached me about this project and helped me develop an incredible vision for this book. I also want to thank my agent, Jessica Faust, who has helped find me book projects over the years and guided me through any challenges. Also a special thank you to my husband, H. G. Wolpin, who puts up with all my craziness as I rush to meet a book deadline.

PART I

Using External Reports to Gauge Your Company's Health and Competitive Status

CHAPTER 1

The Key Financial Statements and Their Starring Role

In This Chapter

- How financial statements are developed
- Who reads them and why
- Accounting methods and why they matter
- Key accounts used to produce reports

As a business owner, you want to know if you've made a profit; the income statement gives you the answer, but is that the full picture? Even with an income statement, you still don't know what your company owns, what your company owes, and what equity you have in the business. You also have no idea whether your company is in a good cash position.

While your income statement shows a profit, how much of that profit actually reflects cash you've already taken into the company? The answer depends on when your accountants recognize the revenue that your company earned. Believe it or not, that can be a complex issue, which we'll deal with in greater detail in Chapter 3.

If you want to review what your business owns and what it owes, you need to turn to the balance sheet. If you want a handle on how much cash has flowed into and out of your business, you need to review the statement of cash flows.

Before I get into the details of each of these statements, let's start at the beginning by looking at what numbers are collected to develop these financial statements. Then we can delve into who reads these statements and why they're interested. Following that, I'll talk about the two types of accounting methods that can be used and how they impact the financial statements that you get from your accountant.

Then we'll take a quick look at the key numbers that are collected and how they're used to produce reports.

Financial reporting gives you a summary of what is happening financially in your company, based purely on the numbers. The key numbers in these reports give you a financial picture that includes the following:

- **Assets:** your company's cash, marketable securities, buildings, land, tools, equipment, vehicles, copyrights, patents, and any other items needed to run a business

- **Liabilities:** your company's debts; reflect the money owed—in such forms as loans, bonds, and unpaid bills—by your company to outsiders

- **Equity:** the money you and other investors have invested in your company

- **Sales:** the value of the products or services that your customers have purchased from your company

- **Costs and expenses**
  - *Costs:* the money you spend to buy or produce your product or service
  - *Expenses:* the money you spend to operate your business, such as expenditures for advertising, compensation for employees, operation of buildings and factories, and supplies to help people run the offices

- **Profit or loss:** the amount of money your company has earned or lost

- **Cash flow:** the amount of money that has flowed into and out of a business during the time period being reported

Without financial reports, you'd have no idea where your company stands financially. You could find out how much money your business has in its bank accounts, but you wouldn't know how much is still due to come in from customers, how much inventory is being held in the warehouse and on the shelf, how much your firm owes, or even how much your firm owns.

WHO READS THE REPORTS?

As a business owner, you won't be the only person who reads the key external financial statements. Many people count on the information your company presents in its reports. Here are some key groups of readers and why they need accurate information.

- **Executives and other managers:** Managers need this financial information to know how well the company is doing financially so that they can identify any problem areas and make any needed changes to improve the company's financial performance.

- **Other employees:** Your workers need to know whether they're meeting or exceeding their goals and where they need to improve. For example, if a salesperson has to make $25,000 in sales during the month, he or she needs a financial report at the end of the month to gauge progress in meeting that monthly goal. If the salesperson believes that he or she met the goal but the financial report doesn't show that the goal was met, the salesperson would have to provide details to defend his or her production levels. Most salespeople are paid according to their sales production. Without financial reports, they'd have no idea what their compensation is based on.

- **Creditors:** Creditors need to understand a company's financial results to determine whether they should risk lending more money to the company and to find out whether the firm is meeting the minimum requirements of any loan programs already in place.

- **Investors:** If you are not the only investor in the business, other investors need information to judge whether your company continues to be a good investment and whether they want to invest more money.

- **Government agencies:** These agencies need to be sure that your company complies with regulations set at the state and federal levels. If you operate a company that sells stock on a market, agencies also need to be certain that your company accurately informs the public about its financial position.

- **Analysts:** If you seek outside investors, they will likely look to analysts to determine whether it is wise to invest money in your company. If investors don't like what they see in the reports, they may decide not to invest. If they have previously invested in your company, they may even decide to sell their stakes.

- **Financial reporters:** If you own a public company, you'll need to respond to the financial press. The role of financial reporters is to provide accurate coverage of a company's operations to the general public. This helps make investors aware of the critical financial issues facing the company and any changes the company makes in its operations. If you own a private company, you have more control over how much information you must give to the press.

ARE YOUR BUSINESS'S FINANCIAL REPORTS PRIVATE OR PUBLIC?

If you're operating a private company, you don't have to prepare external reports, except for those required by the government, such as the financial statement that you include in your business tax return. If you plan to raise additional cash by enticing investors or by borrowing funds, however, you will need to produce three key financial statements for external readers. Whether these statements must be released to the public depends on your business's structure.

Most small businesses are private companies, so they need to provide these statements only to a small group of stakeholders: managers, investors, suppliers, vendors, and the financial institutions with which they do business. As long as your company doesn't sell shares of stock to the general public, you don't have to make your financial statements public. Some companies, such as Publix Super Markets, are semiprivate. Although Publix stock is available only to employees, the company still has more than 85,000 common shareholders.

But if you do sell stock on a public market, such as the New York Stock Exchange or NASDAQ, you are considered a public company and you are required to file a series of reports with the Securities and Exchange Commission (SEC) or with the state in which you incorporate the business each year. Whether you file with the SEC or your state depends on the number of investors your company has. If your company has at least 500 investors or at least $10 million in assets, you'll have to file your financial statements with the SEC. Smaller companies that have incorporated and sold stock must report to the state in which they incorporated, but they aren't required to file with the SEC.

FILLING THE GAAP

Even if your company doesn't need to make its financial reports public, if you want to raise cash outside a very small circle of friends, you will need to prepare financial statements and have a certified public accountant (CPA) audit them or certify that the financial statements meet the requirements of the generally accepted accounting principles (GAAP). Few banks consider loaning large sums of money to businesses without audited financial statements. Investors who aren't involved in the daily management of a business also usually require audited financial statements.

To meet the demands of GAAP, financial reporting must be relevant, reliable, consistent, and presented in a way that allows the report reader to compare the results with those from prior years, as well as with other companies' financial results. Your accountant (whether he works full time for your company as an employee or is an outside contractor) will be aware of these rules and prepare your financial statements based on these rules, which take up hundreds of thousands of pages. A detailed discussion of GAAP is beyond the scope of this book, but if you want to learn more, visit the website of the Financial Accounting Services Advisory Board (www.fasab.gov/accounting-standards/authoritative-source-of-gaap). Let's take a quick a look at the accountant's role in the production of financial statements and discuss where you fit in.

The Accountant's Role

Accountants have a language of their own. As a business owner you need to understand their language so that you can have a better grasp of how they develop your company's financial statements and keep your business's books.

Officially, there are two types of accounting methods that dictate how a company's transactions can be tracked: cash-basis accounting and accrual accounting. The key difference between the two methods impacts how the company records cash coming into and going out of the business. That simple difference can give a company a lot of room for error—or manipulation. In fact, many of the major corporations involved in financial scandals over the past few years have gotten in trouble because they played games with the nuts and bolts of their accounting methods.

Cash-Basis Accounting

The simplest method is called cash-basis accounting. When using this method, companies record expenses in financial accounts when the cash is actually paid out. They record revenue in the books when they actually receive cash in hand or deposit payments in their bank accounts.

For example, suppose your company contracts construction work. You complete a project on December 30, 2011, but don't get paid for it until after your customer inspects the work on January 5, 2012. Using cash-basis accounting, you wouldn't actually enter those earnings into your books until 2012, even though you completed the work in 2011.

Smaller companies that haven't formally incorporated, as well as most sole proprietors, use cash-basis accounting because the system is easier for them to use on their own, meaning they don't have to hire a large accounting staff.

Accrual Accounting

Accrual accounting is much more complex when it comes to recognizing revenue and expenses, but as your company grows, this method becomes a necessity. With accrual accounting your company records revenue when the actual transaction has been completed (such as the completion of work specified in a contract agreement between the company and its customer), not when your company has received the cash. So with accrual accounting, your accountant or bookkeeper may record revenue even though your company hasn't yet received payment.

Using the same construction contract example from earlier, if your company is using accrual accounting, your accountant would record the revenue upon contract completion on December 30, 2011, even though the customer has not yet paid for the work. Your bottom line at the end of 2011 would look a lot better with that additional revenue.

Expenses are handled in the same way. Your accountant records any expenses when they're incurred, even if your company hasn't paid for the supplies yet. For example, when the company in this example buys materials to complete the construction work, it likely does so on account with its supplier. It may not have to pay that supplier for 30 days or more after it has received the bill. With accrual accounting it would recognize the expense as soon as the supplies have been received and record the bill in an account called accounts payable. If using the cash-basis method, however, the company would not record the expense until cash has actually been paid out.

WHY ACCOUNTING METHOD MATTERS TO YOUR BOTTOM LINE

Whether your company uses the cash-basis method or the accrual method, accounting can have a major impact on the total revenue your company reports. The method chosen also has an impact on the expenses subtracted from revenue to get the bottom line. With cash-basis accounting, expenses and revenues aren't carefully matched on a month-to-month basis. Expenses aren't recognized until the money has actually been paid out, even if the expenses were incurred in previous months. Also, revenues earned in previous months aren't recognized until the cash has actually been received. Nonetheless, cash-basis accounting has one big benefit: It excels in tracking the actual cash available.

When your company adopts the accrual accounting method, expenses and revenue are better matched. This provides you with a better idea of how much your company is spending to operate each month and how much profit your company is making. Your accountant will record expenses (also known as accruing expenses) in the month they were incurred, even if you haven't yet paid the cash. Your accountant will record revenues when a project has been completed, a product has been shipped, or a service has been provided, even if your company has not received a cash payment from the customer. Now let's turn to how this information is actually added to the books.

DECIPHERING DOUBLE-ENTRY ACCOUNTING

A key concept that you'll need to become familiar with when talking to your accountant is double-entry accounting. Every time your accountant enters information about a financial transaction, it impacts at least two accounts in your company's books.

For example, if you buy office supplies, an entry will be made in the books to increase the value of the office supply account to reflect expenses paid out for new supplies on hand. That entry will be balanced with an entry to decrease the value of the cash account, so the books will reflect the money paid out. If you paid for the supplies on account, then instead of decreasing the cash account, you'll be increasing the accounts payable account, which allows you to track an outstanding debt that you will need to pay in the future.

This may all sound very confusing, but at least 95 percent of businesses in the United States use double-entry accounting, whether they use the cash-basis or accrual accounting method. It's the only way a business can be certain that it has considered both sides of every transaction.

These double entries are done by entering debits and credits into the books. Each time a financial transaction is entered, the debits and credits must equal each other to ensure that the books will balance at the end of the reporting period.

Now things get even trickier. You probably think of the word *debit* as a reduction in your cash. Most nonaccountants see debits only when they take money out of their bank accounts. The word *credit* likely has a more positive connotation in your mind. The most familiar type of credit may be the one you see when you return an item to a store and your account is credited.

Forget everything you think you know about debits and credits! You're going to have to erase these assumptions from your mind to understand double-entry accounting. A credit may be added to or subtracted from an account, depending on the type of account. The same is true with debits; sometimes they add to an account, and sometimes they subtract from an account.

For example, if a company buys office furniture with cash, the value of the office furniture account increases, while the value of the cash account decreases. If the company purchases $300 of new furniture, here's how it records the transaction on its books:

Account	Debit	Credit
Office furniture	$300	
Cash		$300

In this case, the debit increases the value of the office furniture account and the credit decreases the value of the cash account. Both accounts are asset accounts, which means both accounts represent things the company owns that are shown on the balance sheet.

The assets are balanced or offset by the liabilities (things the company owes) and the equity (claims the owners or shareholders have against the company's assets, such as shares of stock). Double-entry accounting seeks to balance these assets and claims against the assets. In fact, the balance sheet of a company is developed using this formula:

$$\text{Assets} = \text{Liabilities} + \text{Owner's Equity}$$

In addition to establishing accounts to develop the balance sheet and make entries in the double-entry accounting system, accountants must also set up accounts that they use to develop the income statement to show a company's revenue and expenses over a set period of time. The double-entry accounting method impacts not only the way assets and liabilities are entered but also the way revenue and expenses are entered.

If you want to track your company's sales for the year, you need to be able to decipher debits and credits. If you think an error may exist, your ability to read reports and understand the impact of debits and credits is critical. For example, anytime you think the income statement doesn't accurately reflect your company's success, you have to dig into the debits and credits to be sure your sales are being booked correctly.

A common entry that impacts both the balance sheet and the income statement is one that keeps track of the amount of cash that customers pay to buy a company's products or services. For example, if a customer pays $500 in cash to buy a product, here's how the entry looks:

Account	Debit	Credit
Cash	$500	
Sales revenue		$500

In this case, both the cash account and the sales revenue account increase. One increases using a debit, and the other increases using a credit. Yes, I know this can be confusing! Whether an account increases or decreases from a debit or a credit depends on the type of account it is. See the table that follows to find out when debits and credits increase or decrease an account. This will give you an idea of how these transactions will impact your financial statements.

Effects of Debits and Credits

Account	Debits	Credits
Assets	Increases	Decreases
Liabilities	Decreases	Increases
Income	Decreases	Increases
Expenses	Increases	Decreases

You may want to make a copy of this table and tack it up where you review your company's financial reports until you have become familiar with the differences. That way you will more easily be able to recognize if a transaction has been entered incorrectly in the books.

YOUR COMPANY'S FINANCIAL ROAD MAP

Every company has lots of accounts. You and your accountant need a road map to be sure each type of transaction is accurately being entered into the right account. Your accountant does this by developing a chart of accounts, which he or she uses to prepare your financial statements.

The chart of accounts is a listing of all open accounts that the accounting department can use to record transactions. The chart should include a description of the types of transactions that are entered into each account, so the accountant can be sure numbers are added consistently throughout the year. All businesses have a chart of accounts, even if the business is so small that the owners don't even realize they do and have never formally gone about designing it.

The chart of accounts for a business can build itself as the company buys and sells assets for its use and records revenue earned and expenses incurred in its day-to-day operations. If you've never seen a chart of accounts for your business, ask your accountant to show you one. Be sure that the chart of accounts accurately reflects your company's financial transactions in a way that will be meaningful on the financial reports. Although the income statement may reflect only a net sales or net revenue number, you can design internal reports that will give you more detail about what is selling and what isn't. But to get that additional detail on internal reports, you may need to make changes in how transactions are being added to the books and into which accounts they are added.

For example, if you operate a clothing store, the chart of accounts could lump all sales into a sales revenue account, but would that give you the detail you need to know what items are selling and in what sizes? You would probably find it more useful to develop numerous subaccounts to track sales in a way that will enable you to make good purchasing decisions. You could sit down with your accountant, talk about the information you need, and develop an account structure that will help you track your sales successes and failures.

To help you become familiar with the types of accounts in the chart of accounts and the types of transactions in those accounts, I developed the following overview of the most common accounts. The chart of accounts can be listed alphabetically, but it is often developed as I did, which is the way you will find them in your financial reports. First will be the balance sheet accounts: assets, then liabilities, and then equity. Then you will see the income statement accounts: revenue and expenses.

Assets Accounts

Assets accounts come first in the chart of accounts, with the most current accounts (those that the company will use in less than 12 months) listed before the long-term accounts (those that the company will use in more than 12 months).

Current Assets Accounts

- **Cash in checking:** This account is always the first one listed. Businesses use this account most often to track their incoming and outgoing cash.

- **Cash in savings:** Any cash your business won't need immediately can be transferred to a savings account that earns interest until it's needed.

- **Cash on hand:** This account tracks any cash your company keeps at its business locations. This includes money in the cash registers as well as petty cash.

- **Accounts receivable:** If your business sells to customers on credit, transactions will be tracked in this account. This does not include major credit card transactions; it includes only those transactions that include credit given directly to customers without a bank intermediary.

- **Inventory:** This account tracks the value of products your company has available for sale, whether it purchases the products from other companies or produces them in-house.

16

Long-Term Assets Accounts

- **Land:** This account tracks any land your company holds as an asset. Land is listed separately from buildings on that land, because land does not depreciate in value as a building does as it ages.

- **Buildings:** This account tracks the value of any buildings your company owns. **Accumulated depreciation—Buildings:** This subaccount tracks the depreciation of company-owned buildings. Each year, your firm deducts a portion of the building's value based on the building's costs and the number of years the building will have a productive life.

- **Leasehold improvements:** This account tracks improvements to buildings that your company leases rather than buys. Depreciation of these assets is tracked in **Accumulated depreciation— Leasehold improvements.**

- **Vehicles:** This account tracks the cars, trucks, and other vehicles that your business owns. The initial value added to this account is the value of the vehicles when put into service. Vehicles are also depreciated, and the depreciation subaccount is **Accumulated depreciation—Vehicles.**

- **Furniture and fixtures:** This account tracks all the desks, chairs, and other fixtures your company buys for its offices, warehouses, and retail stores. These assets also are depreciated and tracked in a subaccount named **Accumulated depreciation— Furniture and fixtures.**

- **Equipment:** This account tracks any equipment your company purchases that will be used for more than one year. This equipment includes computers, copiers, cash registers, and any other equipment needs specific to your business. The depreciation subaccount is **Accumulated depreciation—Equipment.**

So far we've looked at tangible assets—assets you can touch or hold in your hand. Companies also hold intangible assets, which have a value that can be difficult to measure.

Common Intangible Assets

- **Goodwill:** A company needs this account only when it buys another company. Frequently, when a business purchases another business, it pays more than the actual value of its assets minus its liabilities. The premium paid may account for things such as customer loyalty, exceptional workforce, and great location. This premium paid is shown on the balance sheet as goodwill.

- **Intellectual property:** This account tracks the estimated value of copyrights, patents, other written work, or products for which the company has been granted exclusive rights. These assets are amortized, which is similar to depreciation, since intellectual property has a limited life span. The amortization subaccount is **Accumulated amortization—Intellectual property.**

Liabilities Accounts

Money your company owes to creditors, vendors, suppliers, contractors, employees, government entities, or anyone else who provides products or services to your company is called a liability. As with assets accounts, liabilities accounts are divided into current liabilities and long-term liabilities.

Current Liabilities Accounts

Current liabilities accounts include money your company owes that is due to be paid in the next 12 months. The following are accounts commonly used to record current liabilities transactions:

- **Accounts payable:** This account tracks all the payments you owe suppliers, vendors, contractors, and consultants during the next 12 months. Most of the payments made on these accounts are for invoices due in less than two months.

- **Sales tax collected:** This account tracks sales taxes collected for local, state, or federal governments on merchandise sold by your company. Your accountant or bookkeeper will likely record daily transactions in this account as the money

18

is collected from sales. The money collected then becomes a liability that must be paid to the government entity when due, usually on a monthly basis.

- **Accrued payroll taxes:** This account tracks any taxes you owe local, state, or federal government entities based on withholdings from your employees' paychecks. These payments are usually made monthly.

- **Credit card payable:** This account tracks the payments you owe on company credit cards. Some companies use these accounts as management tools for tracking employee activities and set them up by employee name, department name, or whatever method your company finds useful for monitoring credit card use.

Long-Term Liabilities Accounts

Long-term liabilities accounts track the money you owe that is due beyond the next 12 months. These include the following:

- **Loans payable:** This account commonly tracks debts, such as mortgages or car loans, that your company will pay over a number of years. Your accountant will set up a separate account for each loan, but it may be shown on the balance sheet as one line item.

- **Bonds payable:** This account tracks corporate bonds that your company issued for a term longer than one year. A bond is a type of debt sold on the market that must be repaid in full with interest. As with loans, each bond issue will have a separate account, but the issues will likely be rolled into one line item on your balance sheet.

Equity Accounts

Not all of your assets involve claims made by your creditors. Your owners or investors also have claims against your company's assets. The equity accounts reflect the portion of your assets owned by you, your investors, or your company's shareholders. If the company isn't incorporated, the ownership of the partners or sole proprietors is represented in this part of the balance sheet in an account called owner's equity or shareholders' equity. Here are the most common equity accounts if your business is incorporated:

- **Common stock:** This account reflects the value of the outstanding shares of common stock. Each share of common stock represents a portion of ownership, and this portion is calculated by multiplying the number of outstanding shares times the value of each share.

- **Retained earnings:** This account tracks the profits or losses for a company each year. These numbers reflect earnings retained, rather than those paid out as dividends to owners, and show a company's long-term success or failure.

INCOME STATEMENT ACCOUNTS

Every income statement starts with revenue earned by the company. Any costs or expenses reduce this revenue. The top section of an income statement includes sales, cost of goods sold, and gross margin. Below this section and before the profit and loss section is a section that shows the expenses. Here are the key accounts in the chart of accounts that make up the income statement.

Revenue

Your bookkeeper or accountant will record all sales of products or services in revenue accounts. The following are the accounts used to record revenue transactions:

- **Sales of goods or services:** This account tracks the company's revenues for the sale of its products or services.

- **Sales discounts:** This account tracks any discounts the company offers to increase its sales. Most companies do not include this account on the income statement but instead reflect its impact in a net revenue or net sales number on the income statement. Often the details of this account can be seen only on internal reports.

- **Sales returns and allowances:** This account tracks returns or allowances given to unhappy customers. As with sales discounts, this number will be not be seen on the income statement shown to outsiders but instead will be seen only on internal financial reports. A dramatic increase in this number is usually a red flag for company management because it can reflect customer dissatisfaction or possibly be an indication of a quality-control problem.

Cost of Goods Sold Accounts

Your bookkeeper or accountant will track the costs directly involved in the sale of goods or services in cost of goods sold accounts. The details are usually found only on internally distributed income statements and aren't distributed to company outsiders. Cost of goods sold is usually shown as a single line item on external income statements, but it includes the transactions from these common accounts:

- **Purchases:** This account tracks the cost of merchandise your company buys or produces. For example, a manufacturing company should have an extensive tracking system for its cost of goods that includes accounts for items such as raw materials and labor that are used to produce the final product.
- **Purchase returns and allowances:** This account tracks any transactions involving the return of any damaged or defective products to the manufacturer or vendor.
- **Freight charges:** This account tracks the costs of shipping the goods sold.

Expense Accounts

Any costs not directly related to generating revenue are entered into your company's books as expenses. Expenses fall into four categories: operating, interest, depreciation or amortization, and taxes.

A large company can have hundreds of expense accounts, so I don't name each one here but rather give you a broad overview of typical expense account categories:

- **Operating expenses:** Most of your company's expense accounts will fall under the umbrella of operating expenses. These accounts can include advertising, dues and subscriptions, equipment rental, store rental, insurance, legal and accounting fees, meals, entertainment, salaries, office expenses, postage, repairs and maintenance, supplies, travel, telephone, utilities, vehicle expenses, and just about anything else that goes into the cost of operating your business. You and your accountant should sit down and determine the level of detail you want to track. For example, if you think you want to get a better handle on postage expenses and which department is using the most, you could set up expense accounts on a department-by-department basis.

- **Interest expenses:** Interest paid on your company's debt is reflected in the accounts for interest expenses—from credit cards, loans, bonds, or any other type of debt your company carries. Your income statement will show interest expenses as a one-line item, but you can set up accounts that will track interest expenses from credit cards, loans, and bonds separately on internal reports to get better control of these expenses.

- **Depreciation and amortization expenses:** Your company gradually writes down the expense of major assets using depreciation and amortization expenses. For example, if you bought a $35,000 vehicle, you wouldn't show the full expense of buying that car on the income statement for a single year; instead, you would gradually acknowledge the costs over several years using depreciation. Your profits would be hurt severely if you put the full expense of a major purchase on one year's income statement. These expenses do not reflect an actual cash outlay in any one year.

- **Taxes:** Your company pays numerous types of taxes, but some won't be found on the income statement. Sales taxes aren't listed in the expense area because they're paid by customers and accrued as a liability until paid. Taxes withheld from employee paychecks are also accrued as a liability and aren't listed as an expense. The types of taxes that *are* expenses for a company include the employer's half of Social Security and Medicare taxes, as well as unemployment taxes and other related payroll taxes that vary depending on the state. If you are incorporated, corporate taxes would be shown on the income statement as well.

Now that you have an idea of what's behind the numbers you find on financial statements, let's take a closer look at the balance sheet and how you can use that statement to gauge the financial health of your company.

TAKEAWAYS

- Learn the language of accountants and the financial statements they produce so that you can use that information to manage your business more effectively.

- Understand the rules and methods accountants must follow so that you have a better grasp of how the numbers are collected.

- Get to know your company's accounts. They're the financial road map for your business.

CHAPTER 2

Balancing the Books

Your Assets and Liabilities

In This Chapter

- Why things stay in balance
- Dates and formats
- Honing in on the numbers
- Testing your company's financial health

Think of the balance sheet as something that shows the net worth of your company. If you were to sit down and figure out your personal net worth, how would you do it? You'd likely add up everything you own and subtract everything you owe. Anything left over would be your net worth.

A company's net worth can be a bit more complicated, because there can be more than one owner. The worth of the assets remaining after subtracting liabilities (or money owed) must be divvied up among all owners. The balance sheet helps you keep track of all these moving parts.

The key is to remember the balance sheet equation:

$$Assets = Liabilities + Owner's\ Equity$$

In essence the value of the equity is the net worth of the company's assets. But those assets will be divvied up among the company's owners, based on their portion of ownership. As the company's assets grow, the combination of liabilities and equity grows in a similar proportion.

To help you understand this concept, let's review the purchase of a major asset on a company's balance sheet. Suppose the balance sheet looked like this prior to the purchase:

Assets		Liabilities and Equity	
Cash	$15,000	Credit Cards	$5,000
Land and Buildings	$50,000	Mortgage	$40,000
		Owner's Equity	$20,000
Total Assets	$65,000	Total Liabilities and Equity	$65,000

The company's owner decides to buy a new car for the company. The company pays out $5,000 in cash for the new car and takes a $25,000 car loan.

Here's how this transaction impacts the balance sheet:

Assets		Liabilities and Equity	
Cash	$10,000	Credit Cards	$5,000
Land and Buildings	$50,000	Car Loan	$25,000
Vehicles	$30,000	Mortgage	$40,000
		Owner's Equity	$20,000
Total Assets	$90,000	Total Liabilities and Equity	$90,000

As you can see after this transaction, both the assets and liabilities have increased in value, but the balance sheet stays in balance. There are two new line items: Vehicles and Car Loan. The Cash line item has been reduced to reflect the use of cash to buy the car.

Now that you have an idea of how transactions impact a balance sheet, let's take a closer look at the rules for developing a balance sheet, how it can be formatted, and the key decisions that impact each of the accounts on the balance sheet. Then we take a quick look at how you can determine a company's ability to borrow, as well as its debt-to-equity ratio, using some simple ratios based on numbers found in the balance sheet.

RULES BEHIND THE BALANCE SHEET

Trying to read a balance sheet without knowing the rules behind its development may make you think it's accounting voodoo. But once you get a grasp of the rules accountants follow, you'll have more trust in the numbers that it shows or you'll be able to recognize a potential problem with the financial statement. You'll also have a better idea of what to expect and be a better judge of whether the numbers make sense based on what you understand about the company's value.

Making a Date

First, you need to know what a balance sheet supposedly shows you. It's like taking a snapshot of your company at a specific date and time. Your balance sheet will show the company's results as of a specific date, usually the end of a month, the end of a quarter, or the end of a year.

The balance sheet differs from other kinds of financial statements, such as the income statement or statement of cash flows. Both of those statements reflect your company's results over a period of time, such as a month, a quarter, or a year. I delve deeper into those statements and the rules behind them in Chapters 3 and 4.

If your company operates on a calendar-year basis, the date at the top of your company's balance sheet will be "As of December 31, XXXX." Not all companies operate on a calendar-year basis, however. Your company can choose another 12-month period for its financial statements, which will be called operating on a fiscal-year basis. For example, many retail companies operate from February 1 to January 31, because they don't want to be in the process of closing their books at the height of their sales year. Many universities choose a fiscal year of September 1 to August 31 or August 1 to July 31, depending on their academic year. This makes better sense for them and their financial operations because their collection of tuition and their expenses for operating the university are better matched based on the academic year. Every balance sheet shows two years' worth of data: the year being reported and the previous year.

If your financial statements are on a calendar-year basis but you think a different fiscal year would give you a better picture of your company's financial results, talk with your accountant to determine whether it's worth making the switch.

Figuring Out the Numbers

Looking at a page full of numbers can be daunting to anyone who's not an accountant or a financial analyst. As those numbers get even larger and your company has $1 million or even more than $1 billion in revenues, the numbers become unreadable if shown to the last penny.

For example, suppose your company earns more than $1 million and your financial statement shows totals down to the last penny, your net revenue could be $1,234,567.89. By the time you have finished looking over all the numbers on these financial reports, your eyes will probably have glazed over. Instead, financial reports are represented in the millions, in the thousands, or however your company decides to round the numbers. That will be stated at the top of the report, such as "in thousands" or "in millions." Suppose your company has millions in revenue and your statement is shown "in thousands." The net revenue could then be shown as $1,234, which makes it much easier on the eye. Pay attention to the top of the balance sheet to see what type of rounding is used. This can be crucial as you start to compare your company's results with those of others. Your company may round to thousands and the other company may round to millions.

Formatting Differences

Not all balance sheets look the same. There are three allowable formats: the account format, the report format, and the financial position format. I show you each of these formats using the same simple numbers so that you can get an idea of what you can expect to see. Of course, real balance sheets have much larger and more complex numbers.

Account Format

The account format is shown as a horizontal presentation:

Assets		Liabilities	
Current Assets	$250	Current Liabilities	$200
Long–Term Assets	$400	Long–Term Liabilities	$350
Other Assets	$100	Total Liabilities	$550
		Owner's or Shareholders' Equity	$200
Total Assets	$750	Total Liabilities and Equity	$750

Report Format

The report format is shown in a vertical presentation:

Assets	
Current Assets	$250
Long–Term Assets	$400
Other Assets	$100
Total Assets	$750
Liabilities and Equity	
Current Liabilities	$200
Long–Term Liabilities	$350
Total Liabilities	$550
Owner's or Shareholders' Equity	$200
Total Liabilities and Equity	$750

Financial Position Format

U.S. companies rarely use the financial position format, but if your company competes internationally, you can expect to see this format. This format includes two key lines that don't appear at all on the account or report format:

- **Working capital:** Shows the amount of money the company has available to pay current bills. This line is calculated by subtracting the current assets from the current liabilities.

- **Net assets:** Shows the value of the company that's left over for the company's owners after all liabilities have been subtracted from total assets.

Here's how a financial position balance sheet would look:

Current Assets	**$250**
Less: Current Liabilities	$200
Working Capital	$50
Plus: Noncurrent Assets	$500
Total Assets Less Current Liabilities	$550
Less: Long-Term Liabilities	$350
Net Assets (Net Worth)	$200

This presentation is actually closer to how I started this chapter. The net assets show the net worth of the company to the company's owners. Now that we have these rules out of the way, let's dig deeper into the numbers behind the balance sheet presentation.

EXPOSING YOUR ASSETS

The assets shown on your balance sheet include anything your company owns. This could reflect cash in your bank accounts, buildings that your company owns, and everything else in between. Let's take a closer look at what's behind the assets numbers on your balance sheet.

Current Assets

This section of the balance sheet shows any assets you have that can quickly be converted to cash and that your company will likely use in the next 12 months. These are funds you'll use to pay the bills over the next year. Cash of course is important, but it's not your company's only current asset.

Cash

There's no real mystery about how one defines cash for a company. It's basically the same thing that you carry around in your wallet, but keeping track of it gets a lot more complex for a company because the cash can be kept in so many different locations. Many companies have multiple locations, and each location needs cash to do its job. For example, your company likely has cash in every cash register if you're operating a retail business. If you're not operating a retail business, you likely have petty cash for emergency expenses managed by each department. You may also provide cash advances to employees for travel and other cash disbursements that must be tracked.

Your company must have a way of tracking its cash and knowing exactly how much it has at the end of every day (and sometimes several times a day for high-volume businesses). The cash drawer must be counted out and the person responsible for that cash must prove that the amount of cash left at the end of a day matches up with the sum that should be there after accounting for any new transactions that happened during the day. Petty cash drawers may not be checked daily but instead proved out on a weekly or monthly basis.

If your company has numerous locations in different cities or states, each location needs a bank to deposit receipts and get cash as needed. So large companies have a maze of bank accounts, cash registers, petty cash, and other places where cash is kept daily. At the end of every day, each company location calculates the cash total and reports it to the centralized accounting area.

Remember that when you're looking at the balance sheet, the amount of cash you'll see on the cash line reflects cash found in numerous locations on the particular day for which the balance sheet was created. You'd have to look at internal reports if you wanted detail about where the company stashes its cash.

Managing cash can be difficult because cash can so easily disappear if proper internal controls aren't in place. Internal controls for monitoring cash are usually among the strictest in any company. If this subject interests you, you can find out more about it in any basic bookkeeping book, such as my book *Bookkeeping Kit For Dummies* (Wiley).

Accounts Receivable

If you allow your customers to buy on credit, your balance sheet will have an accounts receivable line. If you do not offer customers the option to buy on account, however, and instead require all of them to pay cash or use third-party credit cards, then you don't need an accounts receivable account. This account tracks the total amount of money due from individual customers to whom your company offered credit.

If you plan to offer customers the option to buy on credit, you definitely need to keep your books by the accrual method, so your bookkeeper will record the transaction in your books on the day the customer actually gets the product or service (see discussion in Chapter 1 about "The Accountant's Role"). The cash-basis method does not provide you with a way to track purchases in which the customer does not pay by cash, check, or credit card on the same day.

Companies must carefully monitor not only whether a customer pays but also how quickly that customer pays. If a customer takes longer and longer to make payments, you must establish procedures for when to cut off credit. Your financial statements might look better with the additional sales, but a nonpaying customer will hurt your cash flow, which means you might not have enough money to pay the bills. In Chapter 7, I show you how to use internal reports to manage your customers' accounts.

Marketable Securities

If your company has cash that it's holding for future use but doesn't need to use that cash immediately, you can invest that cash in another type of liquid asset. As long as the asset can easily be converted to cash, it will be considered a current asset. This can include stocks, bonds, and other securities that are bought and sold daily. You would find all these types of assets on your balance sheet as marketable securities.

Marketable securities is a one-line item, so if you want to know the details about what securities your company owns, you'll need to ask your accountant for an internal report. Your company must report these assets at their fair value based on the market value of the stock or bond on the day the company prepared its balance sheet. So if it was a down day on the stock or bond markets, the value could be lower than it is the day you view your balance sheet. The opposite can also be true: The balance sheet number could be higher than current value if the stock market dropped after that date.

You can get an idea of the difference between what your company paid for these securities and what they were worth on the day the balance sheet snapshot was taken by looking at a line item called unrealized losses or gains. The line item reflects the value of a holding that hasn't been sold, which allows you to see the impact of those losses or gains on the company's value. Many times the line item you see on the balance sheet will show the net marketable value. If that's the case, what you're seeing is the book value of the securities adjusted for any gains or losses that haven't been realized. To get the detail of unrealized gains or losses, you'll need to ask for an internal report from your accountant.

Inventory

The value of products that your company holds for sale will be shown on the inventory line of the balance sheet. The inventory number on the balance sheet shows the value of the products based on the cost the company paid for those products. The inventory line item does not show the value of the inventory at the price you hope to sell the product. In fact, the value of inventory assets can be calculated using five different accounting methods to track your company's inventory value. The method chosen can significantly impact the bottom line. I take a closer look at managing inventory and its impact on your company's financial results in Chapter 6.

In this chapter I want to introduce the key differences in how the value of inventory can be shown on the balance sheet. Here are the five key methods of valuing inventory:

1. **First in, first out (FIFO):** If your company uses this system, your accountant makes the assumption that the oldest goods

are sold first. Companies that use this method usually are concerned about spoilage or obsolescence. For example, grocery stores use FIFO because the older items must be sold first or they will spoil. Software or hardware computer companies will likely use this method because their products become outdated quickly. Assuming that older goods cost less than newer goods, FIFO makes the bottom line of your income statement look better, because the lowest cost is assigned to the goods sold, increasing the net profit from sales.

2. **Last in, first out (LIFO):** If your accountant assumes that the newest inventory is sold first, he or she will use this method of valuing inventory. Companies that sell products that don't spoil or quickly become obsolete may decide to use this system. For example, hardware stores, which sell nonperishable types of products, such as hammers, nails, and screws, can choose to use LIFO. The bottom line of your income statement can be affected if the cost of the products your company sells continually rises. With this system, the most expensive goods that come in most recently are assumed to be the first sold. LIFO increases the cost of goods figure on your income statement, which in turn lowers the net income from sales. It can provide a tax benefit because the lower your profit, the less you'll have to pay in taxes.

3. **Average costing:** The simplest way to value your inventory is the average costing system, which can give you the most accurate picture of your inventory's cost trends. Each time your company gets a new shipment of inventory, the bookkeeper calculates an average cost for each product by adding in the cost of the new inventory. If you operate a business in which the cost of your inventory fluctuates regularly both up and down, average costing can help level out the peaks and valleys of inventory costs throughout the year. For example, gas station operators may choose to use this system because the price of gasoline rises or falls every time the gas station owner takes a new delivery from a fuel supplier.

4. **Specific identification:** If your company sells products that are unique, the specific identification system will be used to track

the actual cost of each individual piece of inventory. For example, auction houses that sell unique items will track their inventory using this system. Computer companies that build custom computers also may use this system. Car dealers are another prime example of a type of company that may need to use this system.

5. **Lower of cost or market (LCM):** If you sell products that fluctuate widely in value depending on market forces, your accountant may decide to use the method called lower of cost or market. This system sets the value of inventory based on whichever is lower: the actual cost of the products on hand or the current market value. Brokerage houses are a prime example of the type of business that might use this inventory system.

Once your company has chosen a type of inventory system, it cannot be changed unless you file for a special exception from the IRS. In requesting the change your accountant would need to explain the reasons for changing systems. Because the way your company tracks inventory value can have a significant impact on the net income and the amount of taxes due, the IRS closely monitors any changes to the type of inventory valuation system your company uses.

Long-Term Assets

Any assets that your company holds for more than one year can be found in the long-term assets section of the balance sheet. Long-term assets include land and buildings; capitalized leases; leasehold improvements; machinery and equipment; furniture and fixtures; tools, dies, and molds; intangible assets; and others. Let's take a closer look at what's behind these numbers.

Land and Buildings

Your company will list any buildings it owns on the land and buildings line of the balance sheet. These assets must be depreciated to show that the asset is gradually being used up. That's done on the balance sheet with a line item called accumulated depreciation. It's calculated by deducting a portion of its value of a company's buildings each year, but the land portion of ownership isn't depreciated.

In times when real estate values are going up, many people believe that depreciating the value of a building actually results in under-valuing a company's assets. The amount to be depreciated is usually calculated based on the IRS's standard, which allows 39 years for depreciation of a building. After that time the building is considered valueless. Whereas that may be true when thinking about factories that need to be updated to current-day production methods, a well-maintained office building can be used for a longer period. A company that has owned a building for 20 years or more may, in fact, show the value of that building on the balance sheet at depreciated value below which it can actually sell the building.

So when looking at the land and buildings value on your balance sheet what you are actually seeing is the original cost basis and the amount that's already been depreciated. You'd need to talk with a real estate appraiser to get the actual market value of the assets.

Capitalized Leases

Not all buildings are acquired by purchase. Sometimes companies enter into a lease agreement that contains an option to purchase that property at some point in the future. If that's the case, you will see a line item on the balance sheet called capitalized leases. When you see this on a balance sheet, it means that at some point in the future, the company could decide to buy the property.

Leasehold Improvements

If your company doesn't own a property but leases it instead, any improve-ments you make to that leased property will be shown on the balance sheet as leasehold improvements. These items are depreciated because the improvements likely lose value as they age.

Machinery and Equipment

Any machinery or equipment that your company owns will be shown on the machinery and equipment line item of the balance sheet. Your account will depreciate these assets, but for shorter period of time, depending on the company's estimate of their useful life. The IRS has lots of rules about depreciation; you can learn more about them in its Publication 946, "How to Depreciate Property," or online at www .irs.gov/publications/p946/index.html.

Furniture and Fixtures

You'll find the value of any furniture or fixtures your company owns on a balance sheet line item called furniture and fixtures. This, too, will be depreciated based on an estimated value of the useful life of the assets.

Tools, Dies, and Molds

If you own a manufacturing company, you likely will find the line item tools, dies, and molds on your balance sheet. This number reflects the value of tools, dies, and molds that are unique to your business and developed specifically by or for your company. This value is amortized, which is similar to the depreciation of other tangible assets.

Intangible Assets

Many companies also own assets that you cannot physically hold in your hand, such as patents, copyrights, trademarks, and goodwill. These are called intangible assets. If your company holds patents, copyrights, and trademarks, they are registered with the government, and your company holds exclusive rights to these items. If another company wants to use something that you've patented, copyrighted, or trademarked, it must pay your company a fee.

Patents give companies the right to dominate the market with a particular product. For example, Microsoft patents its software products and dominates the market with its Windows software and other products it develops for computers or mobile devices. Publishers or authors will get copyrights for any books they publish, so they will have the exclusive right to print and sell those books. Trademarks can be designs, images, logos, names, phrases, symbols, words, or some combination of these elements that uniquely identifies your products or brand. Your company can file suit to prevent unauthorized use of its trademarks if you have registered them with the government.

Goodwill is a different type of asset, reflecting things like the value of a company's locations, customer base, and consumer loyalty. You will see this line item on a balance sheet only if your company bought another company for a price higher than the value of its assets minus its liabilities. The premium your company paid to buy that company will be shown on the balance in a line item called goodwill.

Other Assets

When you see other assets listed on a balance sheet, think of it as a miscellaneous line for items that don't fit into one of the balance sheet's other categories. The items shown in this category vary by company. Some firms group both tangible and intangible assets in this category. Other companies may put companies it owns in full or in part in this line item.

LIABILITIES—THINGS YOUR COMPANY OWES

When your company spends money it doesn't have, the transaction becomes a liability. Liabilities can include credit cards; items bought on account; long-term loans, such as mortgages; and bonds. Let's take a closer look at what's behind the numbers in the liabilities section of a balance sheet.

Current Liabilities

Any liabilities you must pay during the next 12 months will be shown in the current liabilities section of the balance sheet. These include short-term borrowings, the current portion of long-term debt, accounts payable, and accrued liabilities. If a company can't pay these bills, it could go into bankruptcy or go out of business.

Short-Term Borrowings

Balance sheet items that fall into this category are usually credit cards or short-term lines of credit. Short-term loans often carry the highest interest-rate charges, so if your company can't repay them quickly, you may want to convert the debt to something longer-term with lower interest rates. If your company is in good financial health, this type of liability should be a relatively low number on the balance sheet compared with other liabilities. A number that isn't low could be a sign of trouble, indicating that your company is having difficulty securing long-term debt or paying its bills.

Current Portion of Long-Term Debt

Any long-term debt payments that must be paid in the next 12 months will be shown in a line item called current portion of long-term debt. This will reflect payments on loans, such as mortgages and bonds, for which only the interest or the interest plus a portion of the principal is due in the next 12 months.

Accounts Payable

Often your company buys its products or services on account with your vendors, suppliers, contractors, or anyone else you do business with, without paying cash up front. These transactions will be shown as a one-line item called Accounts Payable. In Chapter 10, I discuss ways to manage paying these bills and save money.

Accrued Liabilities

This line item will show any liabilities that your company has accrued (collected from others, such as withholding taxes or sales taxes, or incurred, such as royalties or payroll due) but hasn't yet paid out the cash for. Your company could show this as a one-line item or might provide more detail with line items such as Accrued Payroll Taxes or Accrued Sales Taxes. If your company doesn't break out these items on the balance sheet, you may need to request an internal report to get the detail.

Long-Term Liabilities

Liabilities that must be paid out in the next year or years down the road are shown in the long-term liabilities section. Long-term liabilities won't throw a company into bankruptcy, but if they become too large, the company could have trouble paying its bills in the future.

Many companies keep the long-term liabilities section short and sweet and group almost everything under one lump sum, using a single line item such as Long-Term Debt. This line item could include mortgages on buildings, loans on machinery or equipment, or bonds that need to be repaid at some point in the future. Other companies break out the type of debt, showing mortgages payable, loans payable, and bonds payable.

NAVIGATING THE EQUITY MAZE

The final section of the balance sheet shows the value to be divvied up among the company's owners. In a small company, the equity owners are individuals or partners. In a corporation, the equity owners are shareholders. If you are a sole proprietor, your equity would be shown on a line item called Owner's Equity. For a partnership, each partner's share can be shown individually or the shares can be grouped in a line item called Partnership's Equity. If you divide ownership into stock, then the ownership will be shown as Common Stock.

If your company goes bankrupt, the bondholders hold first claim on any money remaining after the employees and secured debtors (debtors who've loaned money to the company based on specific assets, such as a mortgage on a building) have been paid. Any money left after paying the attorney goes to the owners of the company.

Retained Earnings

At the end of the year, you can do one of two things with the profits: You can pay them out in dividends to the owners or you can reinvest them into the company. Any profit not paid to the owners over the years is accumulated in an account called Retained Earnings. This line item will show you have much you've reinvested into the company since it was formed.

TESTING LIQUIDITY

Bankers or others considering extending your company a line of credit (such as a vendor or supplier) use the balance sheet to test a company's ability to make payments before deciding whether to provide a loan. Investors also use these liquidity tests to decide whether your company is a good investment. Three common liquidity ratios used by bankers and investors to make decisions include the current ratio, the quick ratio, and the debt-to-equity ratio. Before you even apply for a loan, test your liquidity and see how it stacks up.

Current Ratio

The current ratio compares the assets your company has available to pay bills over the next 12 months with the liabilities you must pay during the same time period. In other words, it tests the balance sheet's current assets section against the current liabilities section.

The formula for calculating this ratio is relatively simple:

$$\text{Current Ratio} = \frac{\text{Current Assets}}{\text{Current Liabilities}}$$

To see how it works, let's assume a company has $5,000 in current assets and $3,000 in current liabilities. Here's the calculation:

$$\text{Current Ratio} = \frac{\$5,000}{\$3,000} = 1.67$$

That number means that the company has the ability to pay its current bills 1.67 times over the next 12 months. Bankers prefer a current ratio above 1.2 before they will consider providing a loan. A current ratio close to or below 1 is a big red flag and indicates the company may be headed for a financial disaster. If the ratio is below 1, it means the company is operating with negative working capital. That means its current debt obligations are higher than the amount of current assets available to pay those debts.

You may think that you want to keep that ratio as high as possible, but investors wouldn't like that. It shows that you're hoarding assets rather than using the assets to grow the business. If you don't have plans to use that money to grow the business, investors prefer that you pay them dividends.

Generally, investors agree with bankers on the low end of the ratio but also don't want to see a ratio too high. Any ratio over 2 means the company may not be using its assets to their full potential. The company should consider investing some of its current assets in longer-term growth opportunities.

Quick Ratio

For some, the current ratio is not a good enough test of liquidity, because it includes assets that may not be easy to turn into cash, especially if there is a downturn in the economy. Inventory can be the biggest problem. Whether a company can sell its inventory quickly enough to have cash for paying the bills can be a big question during a recession. A stricter measure of liquidity used by banks and investors is the quick ratio, which is also known as the acid-test ratio.

To determine the quick ratio, you need to complete a two-step process. Step 1 determines the quick assets that will be used. Step 2 calculates the quick ratio.

The formulas for these two steps are:

1. Determine the quick assets by adding these balance sheet line items: Cash + Accounts Receivable + Marketable Securities
2. Calculate the quick ratio by dividing the quick assets by the current liabilities.

To see how this works, let's assume a company's balance sheet shows Cash of $1,500, Accounts Receivable of $2,000 and Marketable

Securities of $2,000. Its Current Liabilities are $4,500. Here's the calculation:

1. Quick Assets = $1,500 + $2,000 + $2,000 = $5,500
2. Quick Ratio = $5,500/$4,500 = 1.22

This means the company can pay its bills 1.22 times in a year. As long as the quick ratio is above 1, a lender will consider the business in a good position to pay the bills. If the number is below 1, it means the company will either have to sell some short-term investments to pay bills or take on more debt until the company can sell more of its inventory.

If you're operating a retail store, you're more likely to see a number below 1, because retail stores carry more inventory than other types of businesses. As long as your ratio is common to others in your type of business, it may not be a problem even if the quick ratio is below 1. But if it does fall below 1, be ready to explain to your banker how you plan to maintain cash flow and keep the business afloat.

Inventory buildup is not the only issue that can cause cash flow problems for both the current ratio and the quick ratio. If your customers are slow in paying their bills, your accounts receivables may also be part of the problem. If that accounts receivable number on the balance sheet trends upward month to month, you need to take a closer look at what's happening with accounts receivable. I talk more about how to use internal reports to do that in Chapter 7.

Debt-to-Equity Ratio

How your company finances its operations can be seen easily by looking at the liabilities and equity sections of your balance sheet. Both sections represent cash that was raised to operate the business. If the cash was raised using debt, the company must pay that debt back plus interest. If the company raised the money by selling stock to investors or adding a partner if not incorporated, then it doesn't need to pay interest payments or pay back investors.

Finding the right mix of debt and equity financing can have a major impact on your company's cost of capital. If you take on too much debt, it will be riskier and it will cost you money. If too much is raised from investors, however, outsiders may think you are not leveraging your assets correctly.

Leverage involves the portion of new assets that you attain for the company using debt. For example, suppose you buy a building with a small down payment and leverage that asset by taking a mortgage. You may have done that in your own life to buy a bigger house than you could afford if you used only the cash you had on hand to buy it. The cash you put down is the equity side of the equation and the mortgage you took is the debt side.

Bankers and investors use the debt-to-equity ratio to determine how a company allocates its debt versus its equity. The formula to calculate this ratio is shown here:

$$\text{Debt-to-Equity Ratio} = \frac{\text{Total Liabilities}}{\text{Owner's or Shareholder's Equity}}$$

To see how this works, let's assume a company has $30,000 in total liabilities and $25,000 in shareholder's equity. Here's the calculation:

$$\text{Debt-to-Equity Ratio} = \frac{\$30,000}{\$25,000} = 1.2$$

This number means that for every $1.20 the company used from its creditors, it used $1 from investors. If the ratio is above 1, it means that the company finances a majority of its activities with debt. If it's below 1, then investors are carrying more of the burden to finance the company. In an ideal world the ratio would be 1:1, but that varies by industry. You can judge how well you're doing by comparing your debt-to-equity ratio with the ratios of similar businesses. Your banker can certainly tell you what's common for your industry.

As your debt-to-equity ratio moves higher and higher above 1, your company's finances look more and more risky to bankers. You'll likely have greater difficulty getting a loan. If you do get a loan, you'll likely have to pay higher interest rates. If your debt-to-equity grows to a level above 2, lenders will consider your company a huge credit risk. If you can get a loan at all, it will be at very high interest rates.

Now it's time to move on to the income statement. I take a closer look at the rules involved in developing that statement and what goes into its numbers in the next chapter.

TAKEAWAYS

- The key to keeping your company in balance is this formula: Assets = Liabilities + Owner's Equity.

- The balance sheet is a snapshot in time, not a summary of operations over a period of time.

- Recognize the importance of current assets versus current liabilities and how they impact your company's liquidity.

- Understand the impact of long-term assets versus long-term liabilities so that you can monitor the ability to keep a business afloat for the long haul.

CHAPTER 3

Gauging Profitability

In This Chapter

- Navigating the income statement
- When revenue counts
- Sorting out costs and expenses
- Testing your company's profitability

Did I make a profit? It's probably the first question you ask yourself when you get your financial statements from your accountant.

The income statement can quickly answer that question because the bottom line shows either a net profit or net loss, but it's not the full story. Looking behind those numbers enables you to find out why your statement shows a profit or loss. You can use these numbers to figure out how to fix the problem if your company did show a loss during the operating period. Even if your statement shows a loss, it may not mean that you actually lost money, because some items on the income statement, such as depreciation, don't reflect the use of cash.

Before we delve into the numbers on the income statement, let's take a look at the rules governing the preparation of an income statement and the data that are collected to prepare that statement. By delving into the data collected for the income statement, you can determine where your business is succeeding and where you need to make improvements.

First, let's look at the four key parts of an income statement:

1. **Net Sales or Revenues:** This will be the first line of any income statement. It reflects the amount of money your company collected from customers minus any discounts given or returns accepted.

51

2. **Cost of Goods Sold:** This line item shows you what it cost your company to purchase or produce the goods or services it sold.

3. **Expenses:** These show you the operating expenses your company incurred during the period reflected in the income statement. That can include money spent on advertising, administration, rent, salaries, and anything else required to run your business.

4. **Net Income or Loss:** This bottom line lets you know if your business made a profit or incurred a loss.

UNDERSTANDING THE RULES

Accountants follow certain rules when preparing an income statement. These involve the date range for the data presented, as well as its format. These approved formats enable outsiders to compare your company with similar companies.

What's Behind the Dates?

Unlike balance sheets, which give you a snapshot of the value of your company on one particular date, income statements reflect the financial activity of your company during a particular operating period. That period can be a month, a quarter, a year, or any other period for which you request a report from your accountant. Some high-volume businesses even review weekly reports to keep a tight watch on revenues, costs, and expenses.

At the top of each income statement you will see the phrase "Year Ended December 31, XXXX" or "Fiscal Year End (DATE)" for statements that reflect a 12-month period. Shorter statements will include their length, such as "Months Ended" or "Quarter Ended," and the date. If you're comparing your company's income statement with another company's statement, be sure you are looking at the same operating period. For example, in a retail environment if you're looking at one company that reports its year-end at the end of December and another that reports its year-end at the end of January, the results could be very different. Although the company that reports at the end of December does include holiday sales, it does not include another strong period: sales during the month after the holidays. This means you're comparing apples with oranges if you use income statements that reflect two different operating periods.

This can be even more critical if you're looking at monthly or quarterly income statements. It's critical that you compare the same month each year or the same quarter each year to get a true apples-to-apples comparison. For example, if you're looking at a December monthly report for one retail store and comparing it with the October monthly report for another retail store, you'll likely see dramatically different results because one reflects the height of holiday sales in December, whereas the other reflects what is likely a less successful month.

Format Choices

Your accountant can choose one of two formats for presenting your income statement: the single-step or the multistep format. Your bottom line will be the same on both formats, but the multistep format will make it easier for you and your external readers to analyze the information. The single-step format is easier to produce. Most major companies use the multistep format, but many smaller companies that don't have to report to the public use the single-step format.

Single-Step Format

With this format your company's income statement will be shown with two sections: revenue and expenses. Revenues can include income from sales and interest income. You'll also find income raised from one-time transactions, such as the sale of an asset, in addition to income from day-to-day operations. Expenses include any money spent to bring in the revenue.

The single-step format gets its name from the need for only one step to figure out a company's net profit or loss—you subtract the expenses from the revenue. Here's what it looks like:

Revenues	
Sales	$10,000
Interest Income	500
Total Revenue	$10,500

Expenses	
Costs of Goods Sold	$5,000
Depreciation	750
Advertising	500
Salaries and Wages	2,000
Insurance	125
Supplies	200
Interest Expenses	150
Income Taxes	250
Total Expenses	$8,975
Net Income	$1,525

Multistep Format

The multistep format is divided into several sections and makes it easier for you to analyze your results more quickly using the ratios I discuss later in this chapter. Although you can use the ratios to calculate profitability even with the single-step format, it will require that you do some calculations first. The multistep format includes four different profit lines:

1. **Gross Profit:** This shows you how much profit your company generated from its sales minus the cost of the goods or services your company sold.

2. **Operating Income:** This line shows you the income your company earned after subtracting all operating expenses.

3. **Income Before Taxes:** This line item shows all the income your company earned before paying taxes, which can include gains on sale of assets, interest revenue, and any other revenue your company earned that is not part of its primary business activity.

4. **Net Income (or Net Loss):** This shows your bottom line—whether your company made a profit after all types of transaction are included.

If you start looking at publicly filed income statements, you may see even more types of profit lines. The most commonly used is EBITDA, which shows you the company's earnings before interest, taxes, depreciation, and amortization. Here's what the multistep format would look like using the same numbers I used for the single-step format:

Revenues	
Sales	$10,000
Cost of Goods Sold	5,000
Gross Profit	$5,000
Operating Expenses	
Advertising	500
Salaries and Wages	2,000
Insurance	125
Supplies	200
Operating Income	2,175
Other Income	
Interest Income	500
Other Expenses	
Interest Expenses	150
Depreciation	750
Income before Taxes	$1,775
Income Taxes	250
Net Income	$1,525

As you can see, both formats give you the same bottom line, but the multistep format lets you quickly see whether you're making a gross profit from the items you sell. Then you can easily see the expenses you incur operating the business. Analyzing these numbers separately can help you get a better handle on what you can do to improve your results. I talk more about how you can use this information later in the chapter, but first let's look at how these numbers are developed.

RECOGNIZING REVENUE: NOT AS SIMPLE AS IT SEEMS

When a company should recognize its revenue can be very complicated. It all depends on how the company makes its money. Although it might be simple for a retail store that counts revenue when the customer buys the product and walks out of the store, other types of businesses earn the money through a means that could take a year or more to actually earn the revenue.

For example, if you're operating a consulting business and sign a contract for a multiyear project, when should you count those earnings as revenue on an income statement? That will be a decision to be made after discussions with your accountant. Not only will that decision impact how the numbers are presented on your income statement but it will also impact when you pay taxes on that revenue.

If you were using cash-basis accounting, you would not recognize the revenue until you actually got paid for the job by cash, check, or credit card. If you were using accrual accounting, however, the rules would get much murkier. I talk more about the differences between cash-basis and accrual accounting in Chapter 1.

Before you sit down with your accountant to discuss when your company's revenue should be recognized, think about these basic concepts for recognizing revenue:

- **Have you agreed on a final price?** If it's the end of the month and your salespeople are trying to meet quota, they may try to add a sale that has not yet been fully negotiated. You can't add a sale as revenue until you have a finalized contract in which the terms have been agreed to by buyer and seller.

- **Have your buyers paid for the merchandise?** Do you operate a business that distributes products to a reseller and then allows that reseller to return the goods if the product doesn't sell? This can be a common practice in some types of businesses. For example, publishers often allow booksellers to return unsold books within a certain period of time. So when recognizing this type of sale the publisher would need to track historical data to estimate a return percentage. The revenue would need to be adjusted to reflect that potential return percentage on the income statement.

- **Do you sell products or services to relatives?** No, I'm talking not about siblings and cousins here but about related companies, such as subsidiaries and their parent company. In this case, revenue is recognized differently as an internal transfer of assets.

- **Does your company work with intermediaries and maintain ownership responsibilities until product is sold to retailers?** This is a common practice when a company works with intermediaries. If the intermediaries don't have to pay for the product until it's been delivered or sold to retailers, then you can't count it as revenue until the intermediaries have completed the sale.

- **Does your company offer ongoing services as part of a sale?** This can be a common practice for manufacturers or retailers that sell technical products that require training, installation, or other follow-up services before the customer can use the product. If these services will be a significant part of the sale, the sale can't be counted until after installation or any other key service has been completed for the customer. If you ship these items to a retailer for sale, you can't count them as revenue until the product has been installed at the customer's home or business.

Your business may have other unique situations that raise questions about when revenue should be counted. Talk with your accountant if you have any questions about when your company actually earns its revenue.

Sales Discounts, Returns, and Allowances

Every business periodically offers discounts to clear out product or accepts returns when there is a defect in what was sold. Whereas the income statement may show only a one-line item called Net Sales or Net Revenue, it actually reflects a reduction in gross sales based on adjustments to these sales.

First, let's look at what's behind these adjustments:

- **Discounts:** Companies offer two types of discounts. One is a periodic sale, such as a holiday sale to attract customers. The second is a volume discount to give major customers a break if they order a large number of products. That's how major retailers, such as Target or Walmart, can offer products at reduced prices; they negotiate a lower price for the products because they plan to buy thousands or more. Volume discounts usually are set based on the number of products to be bought. For example, a product could be sold at $10 to a small retailer and $9 if a retailer will buy at least 1,000 at a time. The discount could extend to $8 for a purchase of at least 5,000 and $7 for a purchase of 10,000 or more. Your company could let all customers know about its standard volume discounts or you could negotiate the volume price on a customer-by-customer basis. Discounts should be tracked so that your business can keep track of sales below full price. If you develop your budgets based on sales at full price and regularly offer discounts, your bottom line at the end of the year will be considerably below budget and your net profit will be below expectations.

- **Returns:** Customers may try to return a purchase for numerous reasons, such as wrong size, unwanted gift, or defective merchandise. Returns are subtracted from gross sales.

- **Allowances:** Many businesses sell gift cards that a customer pays for up front without actually taking any merchandise in exchange. These are called allowances and actually represent a liability to the store. The store hasn't yet exchanged the merchandise, so the sale isn't complete. Allowances are subtracted from gross sales.

You won't see these details on an income statement, so it's important to ask your accountant for an internal report that tracks these numbers on a month-to-month basis; this will allow you to spot trends. If you find you are having to offer your products at greater and greater discounts, you need to dig into why that's happening. Ask yourself whether the market is weakening. If so, you may need to adjust your expected revenue and possibly reduce staff. The quicker you catch the problem, the faster you can make adjustments to your business's operations and reduce your losses.

If you find your returns climb month to month, you'll need to investigate the reasons. This could be a sign that there is a defect in one of your products. The faster you catch that and fix the problem, the better your year-end results will be. You should also be sure any internal procedures for accepting returns are being followed.

I talk about discounts and special pricing and how to get a handle on how they impact your profitability in Chapter 8.

TRACKING COST OF GOODS OR SERVICES SOLD

Every business incurs costs for the products or services that it sells. Even if you operate a consulting business and don't sell a product, you will incur costs to provide your services. These costs are reflected in a one-line item on the income statement. You won't see the details unless you ask for an internal report from your accountant, but the information is collected after every transaction that impacts your cost of goods or services.

For example, when you buy products to sell, the purchase is entered into a purchases account. If you get a discount on buying these items, that discount is recorded in a purchase discount account. Freight costs are tracked in a separate account as well. That way a company can get a handle on the trends for each of these key components of costs your company incurs. If the costs of your purchases trend upward each month, the sooner you know that the better; then you can make adjustments to your business to preserve expected profits.

If you find the price of your products increases month to month, you may need to negotiate a better deal or find a new supplier. If you can't find a better deal, you may need to adjust the price you charge your customers or reduce your profit expectations. The sooner you recognize the problem, the faster you can correct the situation before your net profit turns into a net loss.

If you're running a manufacturing firm, the details for the cost of goods sold will be much more complicated. Not only will you need to account for the raw materials you purchase to make your products, but you'll also need to track the costs of manufacturing the product. That will include the costs of equipment you use to manufacture the product plus the cost of labor.

I talk more about getting a handle on manufacturing costs in Chapter 9 and help you develop internal reports to track your inventory costs and make decisions on how to preserve your profit level.

WHY GROSS PROFIT IS IMPORTANT

After showing your company's net sales or revenue and its cost of goods sold, the multistep income statement will have a line item called Gross Profit. This is simply a calculation of net revenue or net sales minus the cost of goods sold. What this number shows is the difference between what your company pays for the goods it sells and the price at which it sells these goods. With this number you can gauge the actual profit your company makes selling its products before deducting the expenses of its operation. If you find this number is zero or below, there is nothing you can do to make a profit. It's just not worth being in business.

Bankers, investors, or other outsiders closely watch the trend of your company's gross profit because it shows how effectively you're managing your purchasing and pricing policies. If you find that your gross profit is too low, you have one of three choices: Raise your prices, lower your prices, or find a cheaper way to get the products you sell.

These are not necessarily simple solutions. Raising your prices may bring in more revenue to pay for the cost of the goods you sell, but if you raise them too high you could lose customers. Before changing your price structure, be sure to do a market survey of your competitors' pricing. You'll never be able to sell your products if you price them too high, unless you offer a service that no one else offers and customers want. For example, suppose you sell high-end electronics and provide training to your customers at no or low cost. That may be enough to justify the higher price and still not lose your customers.

You may think it sounds counterintuitive to lower your prices to bring in more revenue, but if your products are priced too high, you may be discouraging buyers. If lowering your prices increases your company's volume of sales, you may be able to improve your gross margin. If your volume of sales goes up enough, you may even be able to negotiate a volume discount and lower your cost of goods sold.

Lowering prices can also be helpful if you operate a manufacturing facility that has a lot of fixed costs that aren't being used to full capacity. If you use your manufacturing facilities more effectively and efficiently you may be able to lower the cost per product. Another option may be to look for a new supplier for your raw materials or negotiate a better contract with your current supplier. Also, don't forget labor costs and the impact on your cost of goods sold.

ACKNOWLEDGING EXPENSES

The next section of your income statement is a list of expenses that your company incurred to operate the business and that are not directly related to the sale and production of specific goods. Expenses differ from the cost of goods sold. Cost of goods sold can be directly tied to the actual sale of a product.

Even if your company makes a sizable gross profit, if you don't monitor expenses and keep them under control, your gross profit can quickly turn into a net loss. Let's take a closer look at the details behind the numbers in the expense section of the income statement:

- **Advertising and Promotions:** This can be one of the largest expenses for any company, but it's a necessary evil if you want to draw customers to your business. Advertising includes TV and radio ads, print ads, and billboard ads. Promotions include product giveaways (hats, T-shirts, pens, or magnets with the company logo on them). If your company helps promote a charitable event and has its name on T-shirts or billboards as part of the event, these expenses must be included in the advertising and promotion expense line item.

- **Other Selling Administration Expenses:** Any selling expenses, including salespeople's and sales managers' salaries, commissions, bonuses, and other compensation, are included in this line item on the income statement. The costs of sales offices and any expenses related to those offices also fall into this category.

- **Other Operating Expenses:** On most income statements, companies don't provide a lot of detail about their other operating expenses not tied to sales. If you want more detail, you'll need to talk with your accountant about getting an internal report of these expenses. In the details you'll find administrative salaries, expenses for administrative offices, supplies, machinery, and anything else needed to run the general operations of your company. Expenses for human resources, management, accounting, and security will be lumped into this section.

- **Interest Expenses:** Any interest your company pays on its long- or short-term debt can be found in this line item. You'll need to request an internal report from your accountant to dig deeper into these numbers.

- **Interest Income:** If your company holds CDs, notes, or bonds, any income from these accounts will be reflected on this line item. As with interest expenses, you'll need to ask for an internal report if you want the detail.

- **Depreciation and Amortization Expenses:** This line item shows depreciation on buildings, machinery, or other items, as well as amortization on intangible items. Details about how these numbers were developed will require an internal report from your accountant.

- **Insurance Expenses:** This number will include insurance expenses for theft, fire, and other losses. Many companies also carry life insurance on their top executives and errors and omissions insurance for their top executives and board members.

- **Taxes:** If your company is incorporated, it will have to pay income taxes. The line item will show the taxes actually paid.

- **Other Expenses:** Any expenses that don't fit into one of the earlier line items in this list fall into this category. You'll find it hard to get a handle on expenses in this miscellaneous category, so if it continues to trend upward, you may want to ask your accountant for a breakdown of what types of expenses are included in this line item. You can always ask to break out an item into a separate line item if you want to get a better handle on any particular expense.

Obviously, you want to watch the trends of all your expense items and always look for ways to cut expenses. Getting control of your expenses will help to improve your bottom line.

Net Profit or Loss

After expenses are subtracted, you finally get to the bottom line of your income statement and find out whether you have a net profit or loss. How can you tell whether your company is doing well or not? In the next section I introduce you to some basic profitability ratios that can help you determine your business's success or failure. In Part II of this book, I show you how you can use internal reports to manage these results and catch problems as early as possible in the year so that you can make changes to improve your bottom line.

TESTING PROFITABILITY

Now that you know the numbers behind the income statement, let's take a look at some tests you can use to find out how well you've done. Three key ratios help you to track your profit trends and identify key problems areas: gross margin, operating margin, and net profit margin.

In addition to tracking your own company's trends, it's helpful to compare your company's trends with those of similar companies. A great website to help you do that is BizStats (www.bizstats.com). Its online tool allows you to find industry averages based on your net revenue for hundreds of industry groups, whether your company is organized as a corporation or a sole proprietorship. You can get average income statement results based on your industry and your organizational structure. The information available for free on the BizRate site is about three years old, but you can pay for a more up-to-date report at BizMiner, the parent site. You can get more up-to-date reports on about 5,000 industries at BizMiner (www.bizminer .com/products/analysis/industry/industry-financial-ratios.php) for $69 to $129, (prices at the time this book was written) depending on how many years of data you want.

I've developed two income statements that I use to show you how these ratios work. You can find them in Figures 3.1 and 3.2. Figure 3.1 was developed using the averages for a business in the general retail industry. Figure 3.2 was developed using the averages for a business in the professional services industry. I use the profit and sales numbers from these two income statements to show you how these profit tests work. I used the same net revenue figure, $500,000, to prepare these income statements based on industry averages at BizStats. The key profit numbers are shown in bold face, so you can quickly pick those out on the statement.

Gross Margin

Gross margin shows you how profitable your sales are before factoring in operating expenses. If your gross margin isn't high enough to cover the rest of your expenses and earn you a profit, you definitely have some major work to do if you want to stay in business. How high that margin should be differs dramatically depending on how much you must spend on goods or services to earn revenue. As you'll see from these calculations, a business that must spend a lot of money on the goods or services it sells will have a much lower gross margin than one with a lower cost of goods or services. Here's the formula for calculating the gross margin:

$$\text{Gross Margin} = \frac{\text{Gross Profit}}{\text{Net Sales or Revenues}}$$

General Retail Income Statement
Fiscal Year-End, January 2009

Sales	$500,000
Cost of Goods Sold	$325,950
Gross Profit	**$174,050**
Operating Expenses	
Advertising	$4,380
Car and Truck	$12,097
Commissions	$4,377
Insurance	$3,235
Meals and Entertainment	$901
Office Expenses	$3,534
Other Expenses	$25,027
Professional Services	$1,607
Rent	$15,096
Repairs	$2,550
Salary Wages	$19,201
Travel	$2,333
Utilities	$7,512
Total Operating Expenses	$101,851
Operating Income	**$72,199**
Interest Expenses	$3,426
Depreciation Expenses	$5,233
Income Before Taxes	**$63,540**
Taxes	$6,477
Net Profit	**$57,063**

Figure 3.1   Retail Income Statement

Professional Services Income Statement
Fiscal Year-End, January 2009

Sales	$500,000
Cost of Services Sold	$50,249
Gross Profit	**$449,751**
Operating Expenses	
Advertising	$5,830
Car and Truck	$17,966
Commissions	$15,232
Insurance	$4,066
Meals and Entertainment	$3,121
Office Expenses	$14,945
Other Expenses	$38,399
Professional Services	$6,876
Rent	$12,718
Repairs	$1,955
Salary Wages	$33,319
Supplies	$6,436
Travel	$9,552
Utilities	$7,637
Total Operating Expenses	$178,052
Operating Income	**$271,699**
Interest Expenses	$2,721
Depreciation Expenses	$8,737
Income Before Taxes	**$260,241**
Taxes	$4,813
Net Profit	**$255,428**

Figure 3.2   Professional Services Income Statement

Using the numbers from Figure 3.1 for a general retail business the average gross margin is:

$$\frac{174,000}{500,000} = 34.81\%$$

Using the numbers from Figure 3.2 for a professional services business, the average gross margin is:

$$\frac{449,751}{500,000} = 89.95\%$$

As you can see, a retail business has a much lower gross margin than a professional services business, which means there is less room for error when it comes to operating expenses. With just a 34.81 percent gross margin, a retailer must keep a very close watch on his or her expenses to make a profit. Also, anything a retailer can do to reduce the cost of goods sold will enhance profitability.

Comparing your gross margin with those of others not only gives you an idea of how well you're doing compared with the average company but also helps you track your trends for sales and inventory costs. If your gross margin is trending upward, you're doing something right. Find out what that is and see if you can make changes that will improve your results even more. If you find that your gross margin is trending down, one of two things are happening: Your cost of goods is going up or your sales are going down. You must identify where the problem is and fix it.

On the net revenue side, you may find yourself selling at higher and higher discounts as the market weakens, or you may find that sales have dropped off. On the cost of goods sold side, you may find the cost has been gradually rising as your vendors and suppliers charge more and more for the products they sell. Look behind the numbers in your income statement to identify the problem; this will allow you to develop strategies for improving your numbers. The earlier in the year you do that, the better the chance of your meeting year-end profit goals. In Chapter 6, I show you tools to test your inventory turnover. In Chapter 7, I show tools for tracking your discounts and special pricing. In Chapter 9, I show you how to get a better handle on costs.

Operating Margin

Watching the operating margin trends enables you to get a handle on expenses you incur operating your business. If the operating margin creeps downward, that's a sign that your expenses are gradually going up. It could have a major negative impact on your business's profit goals for the year unless you find out why and fix it. Here's how you calculate operating margin:

$$\text{Operating Margin} = \frac{\text{Operating Income}}{\text{Net Sales or Revenues}}$$

Using the numbers from Figure 3.1 for a general retail business the average operating margin is:

$$\frac{72,199}{500,000} = 14.44\%$$

Using the numbers from Figure 3.2 for a professional services business the average operating margin is:

$$\frac{271,699}{500,000} = 54.34\%$$

Maintaining or raising your operating margin can go a long way to meeting or exceeding profit goals. As you can see, a professional services business has greater potential profit, but its operating expenses are higher than those of a retail business. The key for you and your managers is to find out which line items cost you the most and look at ways of getting those items under control. I take a closer look at this in Chapter 5 and show how to use your budget to get a handle on rising expenses quickly.

Net Profit Margin

Your net profit margin shows you how much you and your investors get to keep for every dollar of sales. Whether you invest that money into growing your business or pay it out to your owners and investors is up to you. Here's how you calculate the net profit margin:

$$\text{Net Profit Margin} = \frac{\text{Net Profit}}{\text{Net Sales or Revenues}}$$

Using the numbers from Figure 3.1 for a general retail business, the average net profit margin is:

$$\frac{57,063}{500,000} = 11.41\%$$

Using the numbers from Figure 3.2 for a professional services business, the average net profit margin is:

$$\frac{255,428}{500,000} = 51.09\%$$

Your bottom line could look great, but your company could still have a cash flow problem. In the next chapter, I introduce you to the cash flow statement. This statement gives you a better idea of your net cash position.

TAKEAWAYS

- Look behind the numbers to find out why your company shows a net profit or loss.
- When comparing your results with those of your competitors, be sure you are looking at the same operating period.
- Get to know when your accountants recognize your revenues and ask questions if you think the revenues should be recognized based on different criteria.
- Carefully watch the trends of both your costs and expenses so that you can quickly make necessary changes to protect your profits.

CHAPTER 4

Cash Is King

In This Chapter

- Why profit doesn't mean cash
- Dates and formats
- Cash activities
- Testing your cash flow

Your bottom line could look great, but does your company really have the cash to pay the bills? You can't tell that from your income statement, because net revenues may not represent the cash you've actually taken into the business and paid out during the previous period.

If you're using cash-basis accounting, that bottom line figure does represent the cash you have, but with accrual accounting you need to adjust the bottom line for actual cash flows. The statement of cash flows does that for you. The reason things become more difficult with accrual accounting is that cash doesn't always change hands when a transaction is complete. For example, when you sell to a customer on account, the revenue is added to your income statement, but you may not have gotten the cash yet.

A statement of cash flows digs into the cash receipts, cash payments, and changes in cash that your company holds, minus the expenses from operating your company. In addition to cash that flows into the company from operations, the statement also summarizes cash received or spent on investing and financing activities.

As you review your statement of cash flows, you should find answers to these key questions:

- What was the primary source of cash for operations during the period shown on the statement? Was it from revenue generated by sales, funds borrowed, or new investors?
- How much cash did my company actually spend during the period shown on the statement?
- What was the change in the company's cash balance at the end of the period?

As you read the statement and find the answers to these questions, you'll be able to determine whether your company is thriving and has the cash needed to operate and grow the business. If there appears to be a cash flow problem, your company could be heading down the road to a financial disaster. Let's take a closer look at the parts of the statement and what they show.

KEY SECTIONS OF A STATEMENT OF CASH FLOWS

When you first look at a statement of cash flows, you'll notice that it's broken into three key sections:

1. **Operating Activities:** In this section, you'll find cash transactions that reflect cash taken into your company from operating activities or cash paid out to carry out your company's operations during the period reflected in the statement.

2. **Investing Activities:** In this section, you'll find the purchase or sale of any of your company's investments during the period reflected in the statement. This can include the purchase or sale of long-term assets, such as a building or a major piece of equipment. It can also include the sale of short-term investments, such as bonds or stocks. You'll also see details of any cash paid out for capital improvements, such as renovations to company facilities.

3. **Financing Activities:** In this section, you'll find any transactions involving debt obligations entered into or paid off during the period reflected in the statement. You'll also find information

about cash taken in or paid out to your company's owners and investors.

The most important section is the operating activities section of the statement of cash flows. That's where you'll be able to determine whether your company is generating enough cash to keep the business afloat. I show you some key ratios you can use to test that later in this chapter. First, though, let's take a closer look at how the statement can be formatted and how the numbers shown are developed.

FORMATTING THE STATEMENT

You and your accountant can choose between two formats when preparing the statement of cash flows. Both formats will result in the same total for net cash, but you get there using two different routes: the direct method or the indirect method.

Direct Method

The rule makers, the Financial Accounting Standards Board, prefer the direct method. This method groups major classes of cash receipts and cash payments. For example, cash collected from customers is grouped separately from cash received on interest-earning savings accounts or from dividends paid on stock owned by the company. Major groups of cash payments include cash paid to buy inventory, cash paid to employees, cash paid for taxes, and cash paid to cover interest due on loans.

Here's how the direct method shows cash flows from operating activities:

Cash Flows from Operating Activities

Cash received from customers

Cash paid to suppliers and employees

Interest received

Interest paid, net of amounts capitalized

Income tax refund received

Income taxes paid

Other cash received (paid)

Net Cash Provided by (Used in) Operating Activities

If your company chooses to use the direct method, it must reveal the actual cash it receives from customers, the cash it pays to suppliers and employees, and the income tax refund it got from the government. Someone reading the balance sheet and income statement can't find these numbers in other financial statements.

So when using this method, you show a lot of detail about your company that you would not want to show to an outsider, but this can give you a good handle on the cash flow of your company. You could ask your accountant to prepare two statements of cash flows: one for your use internally and one that will be shown to outsiders. Let's take a look at the indirect method so you can see why that method is preferred for external statements by 90 percent of companies today.

Indirect Method

The indirect method focuses on the differences between net income and net cash flows from operations. By using this method, your company can reveal less information to outsiders and keep your competitors guessing about a lot of key details. The indirect method is easier to prepare. Here's what is shown:

Cash Flows from Operating Activities

Net income (loss)

Adjustments to reconcile net income (loss) to net cash provided by (used in) operating activities:

Depreciation and amortization

Provision for deferred taxes

Decrease (increase) in accounts receivable

Decrease (increase) in inventories

Decrease (increase) in prepaid expenses

Decrease (increase) in accounts payable

Increase (decrease) in other current liabilities

Exchange (gain) loss

Net Cash Provided by (Used in) Operating Activities

As you can see, when you use the indirect method your company is not revealing any more information than what can be attained by reading the income statement and balance sheet. Essentially all the adjustments to reconcile the net income or loss to the net cash are calculated using the current period's balance sheet and income statement data compared with those of the prior period. For example, if you were preparing a statement of cash flows for the year ended 2011, you would also need to see the balance sheet and income statement for 2010. To calculate a decrease or increase in accounts receivable, you would subtract the 2010 line item accounts receivable from the 2011 line item accounts receivable to determine whether there was an increase or decrease in that line item. I take a closer look at what these differences mean to your cash position later, but first let's look at the other two parts, which are the same whether you are using the direct method or indirect method for the statement of cash flows.

REVIEWING INVESTING AND FINANCING ACTIVITIES

You take a closer look at how you raised or used cash through your investing activities in the next section of the cash flow statement called cash from investing activities. The third and final section reviews your cash flows from financing activities, primarily focusing on borrowing. Here's the key information you'll find in those sections.

Cash from Investing Activities

In this part of the statement of cash flows you'll see detail about the following:

- Additions (sale) of property, plant, and equipment
- Investments and acquisitions
- Sales of investments
- Other

The bottom line of this part is the net cash utilized for investing activities.

Cash Flows from Financing Activities

In this part of the statement of cash flows you'll see detail about the following:

- Proceeds from borrowing
- Net proceeds from repayments
- Purchase or sale of common stock (if incorporated)
- Stock option transactions (if incorporated)
- Dividends paid (if incorporated)
- Net cash provided (utilized) by financing activities
- Cash and short-term investments at the beginning of the year
- Cash and short-term investments at the end of the year

Now that we know what line items to expect on a statement of cash flows, let's take a look behind the scenes to find out how these line items are developed.

LOOKING BEHIND THE NUMBERS FOR OPERATING ACTIVITIES

You find out how much cash actually flowed into and out of your business from day-to-day operating activities in this section of the statement of cash flows. Cash is the lifeblood of any business. If you don't have cash to pay the bills, you won't be able to pay your employees, you won't be able to buy more inventory, and you won't be able to pay the rent on your stores or offices—so you won't stay in business for long.

If your company isn't generating enough cash from its operations, failure is just around the corner. Although it's true that new businesses don't generate a lot of cash in their early years, they need to find a way to generate cash from operating activities quickly or they'll go bust. That's exactly what we saw with the crash of Internet companies in the early 2000s. Many of these newly minted dot-coms got lots of cash from investors, even though they hadn't figured out a way to generate revenue from their operations. When the investor cash dried up, these companies all went bust.

If you're using the direct method, you can quickly get the answers about whether you're generating enough cash from operating activities. But you need to know a bit more about accounting to understand how the adjustments to the operating section impact your cash flow when reading a statement of cash flows developed using the indirect method.

The primary purpose of the operating activities section of the indirect method is to adjust the net income by adding or subtracting entries that were made according to the rules of accrual accounting that may or may not actually require the use of cash. Let's take a closer look at this accounting voodoo to see how the accrual accounting methods relate to actual cash flow.

Depreciation

When your company buys new equipment or builds new facilities, these costs are gradually subtracted over a number of years from your income statement using a line item called depreciation expenses, which lowers your net income. The good news from the cash perspective is that your company didn't pay out any cash for these depreciation expenses, so your net cash is actually higher than your net income shows.

For example, if your company's net income is $100,000 for the year and its depreciation expenses are $25,000, on the statement $25,000 will be added back in to find the net cash from operations. Essentially, from this calculation your company is in better shape than it looked to be before the adjusting for depreciation expenses.

Inventory

An adjustment to the cash flow statement based on the inventory line item can be good news or bad news for your company's cash position. If your inventory number decreased, that's good news. It means that some of the inventory you sold was based on inventory purchased in the previous period and you added cash to the mix.

But if your inventory line item increased, that's bad news for your cash position because you paid out cash and hadn't yet sold the merchandise. If your company's inventory has increased from the previous year, then the company is spending more money on inventory in the current year. So in this scenario you would need to subtract the difference from the net income to find out how much cash your company actually has on hand.

For example, if inventory decreases by $20,000, the company adds that amount to net cash on the statement of cash flows. But if the inventory increases by $20,000, then you subtract that money from net income to find your cash position.

Accounts Receivable

The accounts receivable line item shows a summary of your customers who bought goods or services on credit provided directly by your company and who haven't yet paid off their accounts. Customers to whom you sold goods or services using third-party credit cards from banks or other financial institutions aren't included in the accounts receivable line item. Payments by outside credit sources are counted as cash, because the third-party bank or financial institution immediately pays you. The bank or financial institution collects from those customers, not you.

If your accounts receivable line item increases during the year, it means your company is selling more products or services on credit than it is collecting in actual cash from customers. When this happens, it means you'll have a decrease in cash available.

The opposite is true if the accounts receivable line item is a number lower during the current year than during the previous year. This means your company collected more cash from its customers than was bought on credit. So this decrease in accounts receivable results in more cash received, which adds to the net income.

For example, if accounts receivable decreases by $10,000, the company adds that amount to net cash on the statement of cash flows. But if accounts receivable increases by $10,000, then you subtract that money from net income to find your cash position.

Accounts Payable

Any bills not yet paid by your company are shown in the accounts payable line item on the balance sheet. This means that cash must still be laid out in the future to pay those bills. If your accounts payable line item increases, your company is using less cash to pay bills in the current period than it did in the previous one, so you have more cash on hand. When accounts payable increases, it has a positive impact on the cash situation for the current period.

Expenses shown on the income statement reflect those that have already been incurred but may or may not have been paid. This makes the net income lower. But, in reality, if cash hasn't yet been laid out to pay those expenses, you can add any increase in the accounts payable line item to net income to find out how much cash is actually on hand.

But if accounts payable decreases, the opposite is true. Your company is paying out more cash for this liability in the current period. A decrease in accounts payable means the company has less cash on hand, so you would need to subtract any decrease from your net income number to find out how much cash you actually have on hand.

For example, if accounts payable increases by $10,000, the company adds that amount to net income on the statement of cash flows. If the accounts payable decreases by $10,000, though, then you subtract that money from net income to find your cash position.

BOTTOM LINE: CASH FLOW FROM OPERATING ACTIVITIES

With all these adjustments, what will you actually see on a statement of cash flows in the operating activities section? The following shows you how one might look.

Cash Flows from Operating Activities

Line Item	Cash Received or Spent
Net Income (income statement line item)	$100,000
Depreciation Expense (income statement line item)	$25,000
Increase in Accounts Receivable (balance sheet line item)	($10,000)
Decrease in Inventories (balance sheet line item)	$20,000
Decrease in Accounts Payable (balance sheet item)	($10,000)
Net Cash Provided by (Used in) Operating Activities	$125,000

As you can see, this company has $25,000 more in cash from operations than the net income that was reported on its income statement. So you can see that the company is actually in a stronger cash position than you would have thought if you had looked only at the net income at the bottom of the income statement.

IMPACT OF INVESTING ACTIVITIES ON CASH

The investment activities section of the statement of cash flows summarizes the purchase or sale of major new assets. This section usually shows a use of cash. Some items you may find in this section include the following:

- Purchase of new buildings, land, or major equipment
- Major improvements to existing buildings or factories
- Major upgrades to existing factories or equipment

- Mergers or acquisitions
- Purchases of marketable securities, such as stocks or bonds

Not all transactions shown in this section drain cash. You may also find some cash generators such as the sale of assets including buildings, land, major equipment, or marketable securities. The primary reason you want to take a closer look at this section of the statement of cash flows is to review the key capital expenditures that impacted your cash position.

You also may want to compare your company's investing activities with those of other companies in the same industry to see what type of expenditures your competitors are incurring. With that comparison, you can see if you're keeping up with your competitors, especially in the area of major improvements to factories and equipment if you are operating a manufacturing company. Although your cash position could be stronger right now, will that continue to be true if you're not keeping equipment up to date and your products are no longer competitive?

You can keep a watchful eye on how your competitors are using their excess cash: Check the investing activities section of their statement of cash flows.

EYEING THE IMPACT OF FINANCING ACTIVITIES

If your company is not able to raise all the cash it needs from its day-to-day operations, then you may need to borrow money to generate enough cash. Any cash raised through transactions that don't include day-to-day operations will be found in the financing section of the statement of cash flows.

Stock

If your company is incorporated, then you can raise cash by issuing stock. When you first sell your stock, any money raised is shown in the financing section of the statement of cash flows. You can also decide to buy back stock. Many small companies are doing this today if they want to take the company private again and get rid of the burden of public reporting. By going private, the company will receive less scrutiny from the government and will have to answer to fewer investors. It also will not be required to file public financial statements, so going private enables them to hide more information from their competitors.

If new stock is sold, then that will have a positive impact on the company's cash flow. If the company buys back stock, that means it has to pay out cash, reducing cash flow.

Dividends

If your company is incorporated, you may share its profits with investors by paying dividends. Whenever your company pays dividends, it shows the amount paid to shareholders in the financing activities section of the statement of cash flows. Your company isn't required to pay dividends each year, but if your company stops paying dividends, you can expect the stock price to drop. When companies that have been paying dividends decide to stop paying them, it's usually a sign of a cash flow problem.

New Debt

Anytime your company borrows money for the long term, this new debt is shown in the financing activities section of the statement of cash flows. This can include the issuance of bonds or notes or it can be in another form of long-term financing, such as a mortgage on a building. When there is an increase in debt shown on the statement of cash flows, it means an increase in net cash available.

Debt Payoff

When your company pays off existing debt, it can be a good sign that your company is doing well, but it also means that your net cash will go down. Not all debt payoff ends in a net cash reduction. For example, your company may show that it paid off notes at 8 percent but then rolled over the debt into new notes, bonds, or a line of credit at 7 percent. If you know your company made financing changes, you'll probably need to ask your accountant for more detail to understand the full impact to your company's long-term financing position.

SPECIAL ACTIVITIES THAT IMPACT CASH

You may or may not see these line items on your statement of cash flows. These line items reflect special circumstances that some companies face. Two of the most common special activities include a discontinuation of operations and the exchanging of foreign currency.

Discontinued Operations

If your company discontinues operations (shuts down a part of its business), you usually see a special line item on the statement of cash flows that shows whether the discontinued operations increased or decreased the amount of cash your company has. Sometimes discontinued operations increase cash because the company no longer has to pay the salaries and other costs related to that operation.

Other times, discontinued operations can be a cash drag because your company must pay significant severance payments to laid-off employees and must continue to pay the costs of the fixed assets related to those operations. For example, if your company leased space for operations that were shut down, it may be contractually obligated to continue paying for that space until the contract is up, even though you no longer need the space. You can mitigate these costs if the contract allows you to sublease the space.

Foreign Currency Exchange

If your company imports its goods or exports its products, you likely must exchange foreign currency. You'll certainly incur costs, and maybe make some profits, from this global exchange. As we've seen over the past few years, the value of the U.S. dollar has dropped, which means it costs more dollars to buy currencies that are going up in value. These values change hundreds of times per day, often in a manner of seconds.

Each time the exchange rate between two countries changes, moving currency between those two countries can result in a loss or a gain. Any losses or gains related to foreign currency exchanges are shown on a special line item on the statement of cash flows called "Effect of currency exchange rate changes on cash."

THE BOTTOM LINE

The bottom line of the statement of cash flows is "Cash and short-term investments at end of year." This number actually shows you how much cash or cash equivalents your company has on hand for continuing operations during the next year.

Cash equivalents include cash on hand, cash in checking and savings accounts, certificates of deposit that are redeemable in less than 90 days, money-market funds, and stocks that are sold on the major exchanges that can be easily converted to cash.

The top line of the statement of cash flows starts with the net income shown on your income statement. After making adjustments from the impacts on cash from operations, investing activities, and financing activities, you adjust the net income figure to find the actual cash available for continuing operations.

TESTING YOUR CASH FLOW POSITION

You can use information from your financial statements to test whether your company has enough cash to carry on. Let's take a look at a few calculations that you can quickly do by using your financial statements to check your cash position: free cash flow, cash return on sales, and current cash debt coverage ratio.

Free Cash Flow

The first thing you want to know is how much of the cash your company earns from its operations can be used immediately if needed. This is known as free cash flow. When your cash flow is high, you have a lot more flexibility to make decisions to grow your business, pay down debt, or add to liquidity. The formula for free cash flow uses these line items from the statement of cash flows:

$$\text{Free Cash Flow} = \text{Cash Provided from Operating Activities} - \text{Capital Expenditures} - \text{Cash Dividends}$$

The "Cash provided from operating activities" line will be found at the bottom of the operating activities section of the statement of cash flows. "Capital expenditures" will be a line item in the investing section. "Cash dividends" will be found in the financing activities section if your company pays dividends to its investors.

You should compare at least two years of free cash flow to determine the trends for your company's cash position. If this number is trending downward and you don't know why, that's an indication that your company is bleeding cash. You need to dig deeper into the numbers to find out why.

First, figure out which of the three numbers had the greatest impact on free cash flow. If the number trending downward is "cash provided from operating activities," that could be a sign of a significant problem in your business's operations. Take a closer look at the operating activities section of the statement of cash flows to see what caused the decreases in cash. Two key drains on cash can be accounts receivable (customers are slowing down their payments) and inventory (sales are slowing down).

If capital expenditures have been high, but your cash from operating activities has been the same or higher, then you don't have a problem with operations. You can always delay future capital expenditures if you need to slow down the use of cash. At least with the statement of cash flows you can see the trend and adjust spending if necessary.

Cash dividends are purely discretionary. If the company is tight on cash, it can always decide not to pay out dividends in the next period.

If your free cash flow number is negative, it means you will need to seek external financing to continue growing your company. This can be a common problem for new companies that need to make significant investments to get the company off the ground. If your company has been around for more than five years, however, a negative cash flow should be a major red flag that needs further investigation.

Cash Return on Sales

You can test how well your company's sales are generating cash by using the cash-return-on-sales ratio. This ratio looks at your company's profitability from the perspective of cash rather than from the accrual based net income perspective that you can find on the income statement. Here's the formula for calculating the cash return on sales ratio:

$$\text{Cash-Return-on-Sales Ratio} = \frac{\text{Net Cash Provided by Operating Activities}}{\text{Net Sales}}$$

You will find the net cash provided by operating activities on the statement of cash flows and the net sales number at the top of your income statement.

To see how this works, let's assume your net sales were $550,000 and the net cash provided by operating activities were $75,000. Your cash return on sales would be

$$\frac{\$75,000}{\$550,000} = 0.136 \text{ or } 13.6\%$$

This means that 13.6 percent of every dollar that your company generates from sales provides cash to the company. This number gives you an idea of how efficiently you are turning your sales into cash. You can test whether you're improving your company's cash return on sales by calculating several years of data. You can also compare your company with similar companies.

Current Cash Debt Coverage Ratio

Next, you want to test whether your company has enough cash to pay its bills during the next 12 months. You do this using a two-step process called the current cash debt coverage ratio:

1. Calculate the average current liabilities. You do this by adding current liabilities from the current year and from the previous year and dividing the total by 2.

2. Calculate the current cash debt coverage ratio using this formula:

$$\frac{\text{Current Cash Debt}}{\text{Coverage Ratio}} = \frac{\text{Cash Provided by Operating Activities}}{\text{Average Current Liabilities}}$$

You will find the current liabilities line item on the balance sheet. The cash provided by operating activities will be shown on the statement of cash flows.

To show you how this works, let's assume a company had current liabilities of $150,000 in 2009 and $155,000 in 2010. The cash provided from operating activities in 2010 was $75,000. Here's how you would calculate the current cash debt coverage ratio:

1. Average current liabilities: $150,000 + 155,000 = $305,000. Divided by 2 would equal $152,500.

2. Current cash debt coverage ratio: = $75,000/$152,500 = 0.49

This number means that only about half of this company's current liabilities are paid using cash from operations. The company will need to generate cash through financing activities to pay all its bills during the next 12 months.

In addition to calculating the number for the current year, you should also do the calculation for the past two or three years to see whether your current cash debt coverage ratio is improving. If you're seeing steady improvement, then your company is on the right track; however, if the number is trending downward, your company could be heading toward a financial disaster if you don't find ways to improve your cash from operations.

Now that we've finished looking at the three key financial statements, let's take a look at how you can use budgeting and the income statement to monitor your company's success throughout the year.

TAKEAWAYS

- Watch to be sure your operating activities generate enough cash to keep your company alive for the long haul.

- Monitor your company's financial and investing activities to ensure that you can understand their impact on your cash position.

- Test regularly whether your company has enough cash from its operations. If not, quickly determine how you will raise additional funds to pay bills.

PART II

Using Internal Reporting to Manage Your Profits and Your Costs

CHAPTER 5

Why Budgeting Is Important

In This Chapter

- Using budgets to plan profits
- Starting with sales forecast
- Determining costs and expenses
- Developing and using a budgeted income statement

Too many companies develop a budget only because it's required as part of a five-year business plan to raise money. Then they file the budget away once the money has been received. That can be a lost opportunity to manage and improve the bottom line.

In this chapter I talk about the importance of developing a realistic budget yearly and then using that budget to prepare a budgeted income statement that will give you the tool you need to track your company's success on a weekly, monthly, or quarterly basis. Most businesses will find a monthly budget works best for them, but if you run a high-volume business that changes dramatically from week to week, you may find a weekly budgeted income statement works better for you. If you own a low-volume business or a business whose volume changes little from month to month, a quarterly income statement might be right for you.

In this book I focus on operating budgets. If your business regularly spends a lot on the acquisition of land, buildings, or major equipment, you may want to work with your financial advisors to develop a capital budget as well so that you can plan your cash needs over a 5- to 10-year period.

WHO SHOULD BE INVOLVED IN THE BUDGETING PROCESS?

Obviously, if your business is a sole proprietorship or a partnership, the key budget decision makers will be the owners. If you're operating a business with key managers who will be responsible for meeting their goals, the best way to develop a budget is to set up a budget committee and enable your managers to develop a budget for their own departments. That way they own responsibility for staying within the budget they proposed. Managers will then meet with the budget committee to finalize their numbers and adjust their initial budgets based on companywide revenue and expenses.

The budget committee will determine final budgets. A budget committee usually includes a designated owner, financial officer, marketing manager, production manager, and purchasing manager. Even before your department managers start budgeting, the budget committee will set parameters for the budget process. If revenue is expected to go up the budget committee will tell managers that they can increase their budget by a certain percentage. If revenue is expected to drop, though, the managers will be asked to cut their department's budget by a certain percentage. The budget committee gives the department manager the power to decide where to make the budget changes within the parameters given, so the manager will have the responsibility for staying on budget.

STARTING WITH A SALES FORECAST

All budgets start with a sales forecast. You need to decide how much net revenue you anticipate for the company during the year before you can start estimating how much cash you'll have to cover costs and expenses. Generally, companies determine whether they expect sales to go up or down in the next 12 months based on a number of factors:

- **Past Sales Experience:** Review your sales during the past three to five years on a product-by-product basis to look for trends. Consider cutting products that aren't selling and adding to lines that are doing well.

- **Potential Pricing** Policy (deciding whether pricing will go up, down, or stay the same): You may be able to raise prices on products that are selling well, and you may need to cut prices to move merchandise that's just lingering on the shelves.

- **Unfilled Orders and Backlogs:** You can use this information to determine which are your most popular items and adjust sales projections for the next year.

- **Market Research:** This includes potential sales and competitive data for the entire industry as well as forecasts for the individual company. Also, you should determine whether new competition could impact your next year's sales. For example, if a competitor is opening its doors near your store or in your region, you need to determine how much that could cut into your sales.

- **General Economic Conditions:** Review how they may impact sales. Research economic forecasts to determine whether a downturn or upswing is expected to help forecast sales potential for the next 12 months.

- **Industry Economic Conditions:** Review how they may impact sales. Research projections for your industry. Find out whether industry specialists project an increase or a decrease in the market for products in your industry and adjust your sales forecast accordingly.

But in the end, the most you can do is make an educated guess about what your company's revenues will be for the next year. Start developing these numbers on a month-to-month basis looking at the prior year's activity and then adjust those numbers based on the factors discussed in the previous paragraphs.

Most companies' revenues go up or down based on seasonal trends directly related to that type of business. For example, a landscaping business in the north probably does the bulk of its business during the months of March or April until September or October. On the other hand, a landscaping business in the South may have steady work for most of the year but will still have increased business during the key planting seasons.

Looking at last year's income statement on a month-to-month basis you can quickly see what the ebbs and flows of revenue are for your business. Use that information to develop a month-to-month forecast for the next year, while adjusting projections for anticipated economic conditions and industry changes. For example, if you anticipate that the economy will fall into a recession, then you need to lower your revenue forecast from the prior year's numbers. Conversely, if you expect a recovery, then you may increase your anticipated revenues. Also, if you anticipate new competition, you'll need to adjust projections with that in mind as well.

Once you know your company's anticipated sales, you can plan budgets for purchasing or manufacturing, sales, and administrative expenses. All these budgets will need to be adjusted from the prior year based on anticipated revenues.

DETERMINING YOUR COST OF GOODS OR SERVICES SOLD

Your next item on an income statement budget is the amount you'll need to spend on goods or services to be sold. Once you know how much revenue you expect to make you'll be able to make decisions about how much inventory you need to have on hand to meet anticipated demand. Planning for that inventory level will depend upon whether you purchase finished goods or manufacture them.

A company that purchases its goods to be sold needs to look only at the key accounts that impact the final cost of goods or services line item on its income statement. These include the following:

- Purchases
- Purchase discounts
- Freight

For these companies the key decision will be how much product to buy. To make that decision, they also will need to review how much inventory they have on hand, which they can find on the balance sheet and the detail behind those numbers. With this information, they can then plan how much inventory they'll need to purchase through the year. As with sales figures, inventory numbers will likely fluctuate month to month depending on seasonal trends.

Determining the budget for manufacturing companies is much more complicated, because owners of manufacturing companies must look at not only the finished goods in the inventory line item on the balance sheet but also the goods still in the manufacturing pipeline to determine the level of manufacturing needed for the next 12 months. These decisions will impact how much they will need to spend on raw materials, as well as how much they'll need to spend on labor to produce their goods. All these variable costs will be dependent on the sales projection. The key accounts they'll need to review from the previous 12 months include the following:

- Raw material purchases and raw material on hand
- Manufacturing labor
- Manufacturing overhead
- Finished goods inventory
- Goods in process inventory

Once they determine what inventory they have on hand and in the pipeline, they can then determine how many more goods they'll need to manufacture. Using that information, they can then develop a budget for the manufacturing segment of the business.

TACKLING EXPENSES

With these numbers in hand, the company can then determine its gross profit margin and figure out whether expense line items can grow to meet increased demand or will need to be cut to reflect lower cash inflow. If the gross profit margin is projected to go down by 5 percent, departments will likely be asked to look for cuts of 5 percent or more from the prior year's budget. If the gross profit projection is up, departments may be given more leeway if they can justify a need to increase their budgets.

Department managers can then work to develop budgets that meet company needs based on gross profit projections. By giving managers a goal and letting them determine how they will meet that goal based on their department's needs, you will give them more ownership of the budgets they produce. With that manager buy-in, you'll have a better chance that managers will keep their departments on budget.

REVIEWING CASH NEEDS

When all the budgets are complete, the budget committee then develops a companywide budget using the budgets from each individual department. Usually adjustments will need to be made after all the department budgets have been compiled. The budget committee will then ask managers to adjust their budgets if cuts need to be made to balance the companywide budget.

Following that, the budget committee will prepare a cash-needs budget on a month-to-month basis. Your financial officer or advisor can then use that information to determine whether your company could face a cash flow problem during the year and in which months. Armed with that information, you can work with your bank to set up a line of credit you can use during those periods or find another source of cash. You also may be able to work out terms with vendors and suppliers to allow extra time before cash payment is due.

TRACKING YOUR SUCCESS THROUGH THE YEAR

Going through all the trouble to develop a budget shouldn't end when the budgets are complete. Use the information you developed through the budgeting process to prepare a budgeted income statement that you can use to see if you're staying on budget or if you're facing problems meeting that budget. The earlier in the year you identify and fix a problem, the better chance you'll have to preserve your year-end profit margins.

You'll probably want to develop both a year-to-date budgeted income statement (see Figure 5.1) and a monthly budgeted income statement (see Figure 5.2). The year-to-date budget will give you the opportunity to compare your company's budget with its actual results, making it possible to quickly see whether your company is on target to meet year-end goals. As you can see on the statements, I added a column named "Flag," where some line items have an ↑ arrow and some have a ↓ arrow as an alert. I use the arrows to help you quickly identify potential problem areas. The numbers followed by a ↓ arrow indicate possible bad news and those followed by an ↑ arrow indicate potential good news. Some companies use a symbol that pops up in an additional column, such as ★ to alert the statement reader to potential problem areas. Work with your accountant to figure out how best to set up alerts.

In Figure 5.1, the year-to-date budgeted income statement, you can see that there are ↓ arrow flags for cost of goods sold and the gross profit percentages. The cost of goods sold is a higher percentage of sales than projected in the budget. This mostly likely is the reason for the lower gross profit percentage. Although the percentage difference is not that high, it's still an indication of a potential problem, and the details should be investigated. Chapter 6 and Chapter 9 will give you tools for investigating this kind of problem.

Looking at the operating expenses section on Figure 5.1, you see the only ↓ arrow flag is commissions, which has a slightly higher percentage of sales, whereas total operating expenses has a lower percentage of sales. At a glance you can pick up the differences that contributed to the lower-than-anticipated operating expenses. You'll see that three line items (highlighted in with an ↑ arrow) show no actual expenses—professional services, repairs, and travel. These expenses have not yet been incurred this budget year. As long as you know they are expenses that usually occur later in the year, there is no cause for concern. If this were your budget, the only expense item that you may want to review is the slight uptick in commissions to determine what is driving that upward trend. Nonetheless, thanks to those missing expenses your bottom line temporarily looks like a nice profit increase. Unfortunately, because you know you will likely incur those

Year-to-Date Budgeted General Retail Income Statement for the Year Ended January 2013

	Budget	% of Sales		Actual Year-to-Date	% of Sales	Flag
Sales	$500,000		Sales	$87,000		
Cost of Goods Sold	$325,000	65.00%	**Cost of Goods Sold**	$57,520	**66.11%**	↓
Gross Profit	$175,000	35.00%	**Gross Profit**	$29,480	**33.89%**	↓
Operating Expenses			Operating Expenses			
Advertising	$4,400	0.88%	Advertising	$800	0.92%	
Car and Truck	$12,000	2.40%	Car and Truck	$2,000	2.30%	
Commissions	$4,400	0.88%	**Commissions**	$950	**1.09%**	↓
Insurance	$3,400	0.68%	Insurance	$540	0.62%	
Meals and Entertainment	$900	0.18%	Meals and Entertainment	$150	0.17%	
Office Expenses	$3,500	0.70%	Office Expenses	$600	0.69%	
Other Expenses	$25,000	5.00%	Other Expenses	$4,000	4.60%	
Professional Services	$1,650	0.33%	**Professional Services**	$–	**0.00%**	↑
Rent	$15,500	3.10%	Rent	$2,500	2.87%	
Repairs	$2,500	0.50%	**Repairs**	$–	**0.00%**	↑
Salary/Wages	$19,500	3.90%	Salary/Wages	$3,200	3.68%	
Travel	$2,400	0.48%	**Travel**	$–	**0.00%**	↑
Utilities	$7,500	1.50%	Utilities	$1,300	1.49%	
Total Operating Expenses	$102,650	20.53%	**Total Operating Expenses**	$16,040	**18.44%**	↑
Operating Income	$72,350	14.47%	**Operating Income**	$13,440	**15.45%**	↑
Interest Expenses	$3,500	0.70%	Interest Expenses	$550	0.63%	
Depreciation Expenses	$5,200	1.04%	Depreciation Expenses		0.00%	
Income Before Taxes	$63,650	12.73%	**Income Before Taxes**	$12,890	**14.82%**	↑
Taxes	$6,500	1.30%	Taxes	$–	0.00%	
Net Profit	$57,150	11.43%	**Net Profit**	$12,890	**14.82%**	↑

Figure 5.1   **Budgeted Retail Income Statement**

Monthly Budgeted General Retail Income Statement for the Month Ended March 2012

	Budget	% of Sales		Actual	% of Sales	Flag
Sales	$42,000		Sales	**$45,000**		↑
Cost of Goods Sold	$27,175	64.70%	**Cost of Goods Sold**	**$30,150**	**67.00%**	↓
Gross Profit	$14,825	35.30%	**Gross Profit**	$14,850	**33.00%**	↓
Operating Expenses			Operating Expenses			
Advertising	$400	0.95%	Advertising	$400	0.89%	
Car and Truck	$1,000	2.38%	Car and Truck	$1,000	2.22%	
Commissions	$400	0.95%	**Commissions**	**$500**	**1.11%**	↓
Insurance	$270	0.64%	Insurance	$270	0.60%	
Meals and Entertainment	$75	0.18%	Meals and Entertainment	$75	0.17%	
Office Expenses	$300	0.71%	Office Expenses	$300	0.67%	
Other Expenses	$2,000	4.76%	Other Expenses	$2,000	4.44%	
Professional Services	$150	0.36%	**Professional Services**	**$–**	**0.00%**	↑
Rent	$1,250	2.98%	Rent	$1,250	2.78%	
Repairs	$200	0.48%	**Repairs**	**$–**	**0.00%**	↑
Salary/Wages	$1,600	3.81%	Salary/Wages	$1,600	3.56%	
Travel	$200	0.48%	**Travel**	**$–**	**0.00%**	↑
Utilities	$650	1.55%	Utilities	$650	1.44%	
Total Operating Expenses	$8,495	20.23%	**Total Operating Expenses**	**$8,045**	**17.88%**	↑
Operating Income	$6,330	15.07%	**Operating Income**	**$6,805**	**15.12%**	↑
Interest Expenses	$275	0.65%	Interest Expenses	$275	0.61%	
Depreciation Expenses	$400	0.95%	Depreciation Expenses		0.00%	
Income Before Taxes	$5,655	13.46%	**Income Before Taxes**	**$6,530**	**14.51%**	↑
Taxes	$540	1.29%	Taxes	$–	0.00%	
Net Profit	$5,115	12.18%	**Net Profit**	**$6,530**	**14.51%**	↑

Figure 5.2 Monthly Budgeted Income Statement

missing expenses at some point, you won't be seeing that jump in net profit at the end of the year based on those line items.

Figure 5.2, the monthly budgeted income statement helps you quickly dig deeper into the differences that could be causing the arrow alerts noticed in Figure 5.1, the year-to-date statement. As you can see in this sample statement, sales are up $3,000 from the budgeted amount. Cost of goods also is up $3,000. Although you might expect cost of goods to be up some with increased sales because the company needed to purchase goods sooner than anticipated to meet increasing sales demand, you would not expect that much of an increase in cost of goods sold unless the purchase price went up as well. That increase in cost of goods sold is what impacted the reduction in projected gross profit.

Commissions are up slightly because of the higher volume of sales, so that's not a big area for concern. The rest of the differences can be explained because expenses have not yet been incurred for professional services, repairs, and travel. After seeing these reports, your next step would be to study the increase in the cost of goods sold.

In developing your budgeted income statement formats, focus primarily on the line items that you want to track. For example, you may want to lump line items in the expense category that are relatively stable year to year in an "other administrative expenses" category on the budgeted income statement. That way you can focus your attention on the critical line items. Line items such as rent and insurance will likely not change much from the budgeted to actual expense, so they can be good candidates for the "other" categories. It's up to you to determine the amount of detail you want to see on a budgeted income statement.

You also can ask your accountant to add detail to the budgeted income statement. For example, you can ask your accountant to include detail from all the accounts that roll into sales and cost of goods sold. By including these additional accounts on the budgeted income statement, you can quickly pick up any change from what was originally budgeted.

Remember, these budgeted income statements will be shared only internally among owners and managers who need to see the numbers.

These statements are not intended for external use, so including confidential information will not be a problem.

Now that I've introduced you to budgeted income statements, let's take a closer look at how you can manage inventory to improve control over your cash position.

TAKEAWAYS

- Budgeting should become a yearly exercise that helps you keep on top of your year-end goals.

- If you have managers who have the responsibility to stay on budget, your best way of getting their buy-in is to include them in the budget planning process.

- Don't just file away your budget after it's been drawn up. Use it to develop a budgeted income statement that becomes a tool you can use throughout the year to identify trends that could impact your bottom line at year-end. The earlier you identify any problems, the better the chance of your meeting your year-end profit goals.

CHAPTER 6

Managing Inventory

In This Chapter

- Valuing your inventory
- Determining its impact on your bottom line
- Testing your inventory turnover
- Comparing your results
- Financing inventory

Your company's primary cash generator should be the goods or services you sell, so you need to keep a close watch on how quickly your inventory turns over and generates cash. Two key line items— inventory (on the balance sheet) and cost of goods sold (on the income statement)—give you the basic information you need to manage your inventory. As always, however, the devil is in the details about how these line items are calculated.

In this chapter, I explore inventory valuation and how it impacts both your balance sheet and income statement. Then I show you how to test your inventory turnover. Finally, I discuss some possible options for financing that inventory.

UNDERSTANDING INVENTORY VALUATION

Valuation of your inventory involves some key accounting decisions. When it comes to dealing with accounting methods, the calculations can be complicated and depend on decisions you and your accountant make. As I discussed in Chapter 1, there are five key methods for valuing inventory:

1. **Last In, First Out (LIFO) Inventory Valuation Method:** This method assumes the last item you put on the shelf will be the first item sold. When you use this method, your cost of goods sold number will likely be higher because the last purchased inventory probably costs more than previously purchased inventory. You can use this method if you operate a business where the age of the inventory doesn't matter. For example, a hardware store likely puts its newest hammers on the shelves in front so the customers will buy those first. The store owner is not likely to unload all the older hammers, so he or she can put the newer hammers in the back.

2. **First In, First Out (FIFO) Inventory Valuation Method:** This method assumes the first item you put on the shelf will be the first item sold. When you use this method, it's assumed that the oldest item is sold first, which is probably the cheapest item in the inventory. You would use this method if spoilage is a big concern in your business. For example, a grocery store will empty its shelves and put the newest milk in the back to encourage the customer to buy the oldest milk out front. Of course, that doesn't always work, because many customers will check dates on the milk and pick from the back. But in this case we're just talking about how your accountant will calculate the value of your inventory, not how the inventory actually moves off the shelves.

3. **Average Costing Inventory Valuation Method:** This valuation method doesn't try to figure out which items sell first. Instead, your accountant will just average the cost of inventory on hand at the beginning of the month and add the cost of any inventory purchased during the month to determine an average cost of inventory. This inventory method gives you a way to watch the overall trends of your inventory's cost.

4. **Specific Identification Inventory Valuation Method:** With this method, the cost of inventory is calculated by tallying the costs of each individual product in your inventory. For example, if you sell high-value items with lots of customized

options, you would need to specifically identify the inventory sold. For example, when you shop in a new or used car lot you likely see a different price on each car in inventory. This car dealer likely uses the specific identification inventory method to calculate its inventory value and costs of goods sold.

5. **Lower-of-Cost or Market Inventory Valuation Method:** The value of the inventory on hand is determined based on whichever cost is lower: the actual cost of the inventory or its current market value. This valuation method will be found in companies whose inventory value changes rapidly, sometimes even during the day. For example, dealers in precious metals, commodities, and publicly traded securities commonly use this method.

The way you and your accountant choose to value the inventory can have a major impact on your company's bottom line. The actual figure you use as the cost of goods or services sold on your income statement depends on the costs you allocate to the inventory sold during the accounting period, whether it's a monthly, quarterly, or yearly income statement. The inventory value shown on your balance sheet represents the value of the inventory you still have on hand. Let's take a closer look at how inventory is valued using these different account methods and how that value impacts the cost of goods sold line item, which ultimately impacts your bottom line.

CALCULATING INVENTORY AND COST OF GOODS SOLD

To calculate the value of inventory during the current month, you start with the beginning value of the inventory on the first day of the month. The beginning inventory number will be the same number shown on the balance sheet as the ending inventory of the previous month. Then you add purchases made during the month. The final number you need is a count of the inventory still held by the company at the end of the month.

Companies use two methods for tracking inventory:

1. Periodic inventory involves counting the inventory on the shelves and in the warehouses. Companies that use this method will do a physical count of inventory regularly, commonly once a month. High-volume businesses may do physical counts at the end of every day.

2. Perpetual inventory uses a computer system to adjust inventory automatically after every sale. When using this system, customers will get a sales receipt with a number and product name for each item purchased. Even a company that uses a perpetual inventory system will conduct a physical count of inventory periodically to adjust its actual inventory count for spoilage and theft.

Whichever method a company uses, it still must know its beginning inventory on hand to calculate its cost of goods sold. Here's the formula for calculating the cost of goods sold line item on the income statement, as well as the ending inventory number to be used on the balance sheet:

1. Find the value of the goods available for sale.

Beginning Inventory + Purchases = Goods Available for Sale

2. Calculate the value of items sold.

Goods Available for Sale − Ending Inventory = Number of Items Sold

Let's do some simple calculations using this formula to see how the various inventory valuation methods can impact your bottom line. I look only at the three most commonly used methods: average costing, FIFO, and LIFO. So you can compare the impacts, I use the same beginning inventory, purchases, and ending inventory for a one-month period. I do these calculations assuming just one type of product to simplify things for this book, but your business most likely has numerous products and calculations that must be done for each. If you're operating a manufacturing company, the calculations are more complicated. I take a closer look at those calculations in Chapter 9, but let's keep things simple for this initial discussion.

Here's the basic numbers we'll use in these calculations:

Beginning Inventory: 100 units for sale
Purchases: 500 units purchased during the month
Ending Inventory: 100 units on hand at the end of the month

Using these inventory numbers, I calculate the goods available for sale and the number of items sold:

Beginning Inventory	100
Purchases	+500
Goods Available for Sale	=600
Number of Items Sold	−500
Ending Inventory	100

During the month, I assume these purchases were made:

Day 1:   Bought 100 items at $20
Day 15:   Bought 200 items at $21
Day 25:   Bought 200 items at $22

The beginning inventory value was 100 items at $18.

Average Costing

First, let's take a look at the average costing inventory valuation method. In this method you start by calculating a value for each purchase separately, as well as the value of beginning inventory. Here's the calculation:

100 @ $18 = $1,800 (beginning inventory value)

113

Plus purchases:

100 @ $20 = $2,000 (day 1 purchase)

200 @ $21 = $4,200 (day 15 purchase)

200 @ $22 = $4,400 (day 25 purchase)

Total cost of goods available for sale = $12,400

Next, we calculate the average cost per unit:

$$\frac{\$12,400 \text{ (Cost of Goods Available for Sale)}}{600 \text{ (Number of Units)}} = \frac{\$20.67 \text{ (Average}}{\text{Cost per Unit Sold)}}$$

Once you know the average cost per unit, you can calculate the cost of goods sold and the ending inventory value. Here's the calculation:

Cost of goods sold: 500 @ $20.67 each = $10,335
Ending inventory: 100 @ $20.67 each = $2,067

So using this inventory valuation method, the number you would see on the income statement for cost of goods sold would be $10,335. The number on the balance sheet for ending inventory would be $2,067.

FIFO

When calculating the value of inventory using FIFO, the first units sold are the first units put on the shelves. So you would start the calculation with beginning inventory, and then add purchases as they were made until you get to the total number of units sold: 500. The 100 units remaining would be from the last purchase.

Here's how the calculation would be done:

Beginning inventory: 100 @ $18 = $1,800
Day 1 purchase: 100 @ $20 = $2,000
Day 15 purchase: 200 @ $21 = $4,200
Day 25 purchase: 100 @ $22 = $2,200
Cost of goods sold: = $10,200
Ending inventory: 100 @ $2,200 = $2,200

As you can see with this method, the cost of goods sold number is slightly lower, which means the bottom line on the income statement will be slightly higher. The value of the ending inventory number that will be shown on the balance sheet is slightly higher.

LIFO

When you are calculating the value of inventory using LIFO, the first units sold are the ones last purchased during the month. So you start the calculation using the Day 25 purchase until you get to the number of units sold: 500. The 100 units remaining will be the ones in beginning inventory.

Here's how the calculation would be done:

Day 25 purchase: 200 @ $22 = $4,400
Day 15 purchase: 200 @ $21 = $4,200
Day 1 purchase: 100 @ $20 = $2,000
Cost of goods sold: = $10,600
Ending inventory: 100 @ $18 = $1,800

As you can see with this calculation, the cost of goods sold number in the highest of the three, which means the income on the bottom line will be the lowest. The value of inventory on the balance sheet will be the lowest.

COMPARING INVENTORY VALUATION METHODS

Let's take a closer look at how these three methods would impact the bottom line on the income statement:

	Cost Averaging	FIFO	LIFO
Sales	$15,000	$15,000	$15,000
Cost of Goods Sold	$10,335	$10,200	$10,600
Gross Income	$4,665	$4,800	$4,400

As expected, the lowest gross income figure results from using the LIFO method. Obviously, this can have a big impact on the bottom line when you consider all the products your company sells. The higher cost of goods will also give the business a higher tax write-off, so that can be a savings as well.

The value of the business as shown on the balance sheet will also be different. Here's the comparison:

	Cost Averaging	FIFO	LIFO
Ending Inventory	$2,067	$2,200	$1,800

Your balance sheet will show the highest inventory value on the balance sheet using the FIFO method in most situations. Conversely, the LIFO method will result in the lowest inventory value on the balance sheet. This will be true for most industries, where the costs of goods sold tend to trend upward, but if you're in an industry where costs are dropping, the oldest inventory could be the highest priced inventory. In that scenario the LIFO ending inventory would have the highest value. In an industry in which costs are dropping, the LIFO ending inventory could actually be valued higher than it's worth.

If you want to get a good handle on what's happening with your cost of goods sold, you can ask your accountant to develop a month-to-month internal report that summarizes your purchases each month by product line. Here's what the monthly report could look like:

	January		February	
	# of Units	Average Price per Unit	# of Units	Average Price per Unit
Widgets	500	$17.50	500	$17.75
Gadgets	400	$15.25	600	$15.25

And so on . . .

This report can give you a quick overview of the cost trends for all of your products. If you see certain products are jumping dramatically in price, it may be time to find a new supplier or raise your prices to maintain your bottom line. Of course, there are many more things you need to think about before making a change, such as: Will the quality of your products continue to be what your customers expect if you select a new supplier? Will your customers be willing to pay a higher price? If not satisfied with quality or price, will they decide to switch to a competitor?

TESTING YOUR INVENTORY TURNOVER

Now that you know how the inventory and cost of goods sold numbers are calculated, it's time for the big test that will help you determine how quickly your inventory turns over. That can be critical to your ability to maintain a healthy cash flow and ultimately turn a profit.

You use this three-step process to find out how quickly your products are moving out of your stores:

1. Calculate the average inventory. This will give you an idea of the average number of units you held in inventory. The formula is:

$$\frac{\text{Beginning Inventory} + \text{Ending Inventory}}{2} = \text{Average Inventory}$$

2. Calculate the inventory turnover. This measures the number of times inventory is completely sold out during an accounting period. The formula is:

$$\frac{\text{Cost of Goods Sold}}{\text{Average Inventory}} = \text{Inventory Turnover}$$

3. Calculate the number of days it takes for products to go through the inventory system. The formula is:

$$\frac{365}{\text{Inventory Turnover}} = \text{Number of Days to Sell All Inventory}$$

I use the cost of goods sold number from the General Retail Income Statement in Figure 3.1—$325,950—for this calculation. I assume ending inventory value shown on the balance sheet at of the end of the previous year was $26,875. This will become the beginning inventory for the current year. The ending inventory value for the current year was $28,325. These numbers would be found on the balance sheet for the previous year and the current year. Let's use these numbers to calculate the inventory turnover and then the number of days it takes to sell all inventory.

$$\text{Average Inventory} = \frac{(\$26,875 + \$28,325)}{2} = \$27,600$$

$$\text{Inventory Turnover} = \frac{\$325,950}{\$27,600} = 11.81\%$$

$$\text{Number of Days to Sell All Inventory} = \frac{365}{11.81} = 30.9$$

So what do these calculations mean? This general retailer sells its entire inventory every 30.9 days. Is that good or bad? You can test your success at turning over your inventory by finding out what is common within your industry at BizStats (www.bizstats.com). By putting in the $500,000 sales number, I found the common inventory turnover percentage for general retail was 9.34 percent. So this retailer is doing better than average, moving the entire inventory on average every 30.9 days.

If you calculate the industry average, you find the number of days to move all inventory in the general retail category is 39.1 days (365/9.34); this retailer is doing considerably better than the industry average.

If you find your business is below par on inventory turnover, it's time to research the market and figure out why product is moving more slowly in your business compared with product in similar businesses.

BORROWING AGAINST INVENTORY

One way to improve your cash position is to reduce the amount of inventory you keep on hand. Doing this certainly reduces the amount of cash that you have to pay out, but it can result in lost sales if customers come in to buy a product that you don't have on your shelves. You can also consider short-term borrowing options for your business so that you can maintain a higher inventory level and be sure your customers find the products they want:

- **Flooring:** With this method you pay for inventory when it's sold. You can't do this in every type of business, but some manufacturers will consider this option, which is like consignment, to get their products to market. Also sometimes you can work out a loan using a "flooring charge," where the lender agrees to a certain percentage based on how long your product stays on the floor. With this type of loan you borrow cash based on inventory on hand and then repay the cash plus a flooring charge once the inventory has been sold.

- **Extended Payment Terms:** Sometimes you can work out a deal with a supplier or vendor to extend your payment terms. For example, if the vendor normally requires a payment within 30 days of billing, you may be able to negotiate a payment term of 60 to 90 days plus interest on the amount due. Of course, you can always pay a bill late plus interest, but you're better off working out terms for delayed payment up front. If you pay late on a regular basis without making arrangements, the vendor or supplier could require cash on delivery for future orders and make your cash flow situation much worse.

Now let's take a look at another prime cash source, accounts receivable. Collecting on time from customers who buy on account can be critical to maintaining your business's cash flow. In the next chapter I explore how to keep an eye on customer collections.

TAKEAWAYS

- Your inventory value differs depending upon the accounting method that is used. Get to know the inventory method your accountant uses and how that impacts your bottom line. If your business is not yet operating, talk with your accountant about your valuation options.

- Inventory valuation impacts both your cost of goods sold and ultimately your bottom line. It can also impact your tax bill.

- Use your inventory and cost of goods line items to test how well your inventory moves. Then compare those numbers with what is common for your industry to find out whether you have room for improvement.

- If your inventory moves too slowly for your cash flow needs, get creative about how to finance that inventory by working out a deal with your suppliers or vendors or talking with your bank about lending options based on inventory on hand.

CHAPTER 7

Monitoring Customer Collections

In This Chapter

- Determining accounts receivable turnover
- Developing reports to monitor customer payments
- Discovering alternatives for speeding up collections
- Borrowing on receivables

Can you collect the cash? If your customers buy on account and don't pay you on time, it can create a huge cash flow problem. Although your bottom line might look great thanks to the sales, you could end up with a cash flow disaster if you don't have the money to pay your bills.

Monitoring your customer accounts and how quickly they pay the bill will give you a good handle on the cash you can count on to run the business. If that slows down, you need to find alternatives for raising the cash, such as borrowing on the money due.

In this chapter, I show you how to measure your accounts receivable turnover and how to develop reports to monitor your customer's payment habits. I then talk about ways to speed up collections if you see a slowdown in payments. Finally, I discuss options for borrowing on the money due to keep cash flowing in your business.

WHAT IS ACCOUNTS RECEIVABLE?

If your company offers to sell to customers on account, the amount due gets tracked in an account called accounts receivable. That line item can be seen on the balance sheet. The detail behind that line item is critical if you want to know whether cash could become a problem down the road.

The accounts receivable line item does not track sales involving credit cards or credit offered by a third party. You don't have to worry about collecting from those customers. You'll only see this line item on your balance sheet if your business sells to customers on in-store credit.

When you sell to a customer on in-store credit, the purchase is entered into the books in two places: in the accounts receivable account and in an account that tracks the payments for each individual customer. The detail in the customer account is used to develop a periodic billing, usually monthly. After the bill has been sent, the customer is given a number of days to pay, usually between 10 and 30 days. You can see how quickly your customers are actually paying the bill by calculating the accounts receivable turnover.

CALCULATING THE ACCOUNTS RECEIVABLE TURNOVER

Calculating the accounts receivable turnover is a three-step process:

1. Calculate the average accounts receivable:
   Add the current year's accounts receivable and the previous year's accounts receivable and then divide it by 2. You can find this line item on the balance sheet.

2. Find the accounts receivable turnover ratio:
   Calculate the accounts receivable turnover ratio by dividing the annual in-store credit sales by the average accounts receivable number you calculated in step 1. You won't find this number on an external financial report. You'll need to ask for it from your accountant.

3. Find the average sales credit period (the time it takes customers to pay the bill):
   Calculate the average sales credit period by dividing 52 weeks by the accounts receivable turnover ratio.

To practice this calculation, let's assume the accounts receivable line item was $35,700 at the end of the previous year and was $36,500 at the end of the current year. I also assume annual in-store credit sales totaled $250,000. Here's how you do the calculations:

1. $$\text{Average Accounts Receivable} = \frac{(\$35,700 + \$36,500)}{2} = \$36,100$$

2. Accounts receivable turnover ratio:

$$\frac{\$250,000}{\$36,100} = 6.93$$

3. Average sales credit period:

$$\frac{52}{6.93} = 7.5 \text{ weeks}$$

So this business is taking 7.5 weeks to collect from its customers. That can be a huge problem if it must pay for its inventory in a shorter period of time. It won't take long for a business in this situation to face a cash flow problem. Even when first looking at the numbers for accounts receivable, you can see that there has been a problem developing in the collection of customer accounts. The current year's accounts receivable line item was higher than the previous year's accounts receivable, which likely indicates that accounts receivable collection is slowing down. In the previous example, you can see that at the end of the previous year the accounts receivable line item was $800 lower than the current year, which means even more customers are paying more slowly or some large customers are paying more slowly.

Whenever you see your accounts receivable number trending upward from accounting period to accounting period, you need to investigate the trend. If your net sales number is trending up and more sales are being made on in-store accounts, that also could explain an accounts receivable number trending up, which can be good news. But it's important to investigate any change in trend.

DIGGING INTO ACCOUNTS RECEIVABLE

To keep your accounts receivables under control, you need to find out what's happening behind those numbers. You do this by asking your accountant to develop an Accounts Receivable Aging Schedule, similar to the following:

Accounts Receivable Aging Schedule for General Retailing Company as of February 2012

Customer	30–45 Days	46–60 Days	61–90 Days	Over 90 Days	Total
Sam Adams	$1,000	$500	$0	$0	$1,500
Barbara Jones	$2,000	$1,000	$0	$0	$3,000
William Jones	$2,000	$1,000	$1,000	$0	$4,000
Susie Landen	$3,000	$1,500	$500	$250	$5,250
Mary Smith	$2,000	$1,000	$0	$0	$3,000
Smithers & Co.	$7,000	$3,500	$2,000	$1,000	$13,500
Wes Wesly	$5,000	$2,500	$0	$0	$7,500
Total	**$22,000**	**$11,000**	**$3,500**	**$1,250**	**$37,750**

Reviewing this statement, you can quickly pick out the problem customers. William Jones is overdue by more than 60 days and Susie Landen and Smithers & Co. are past due by more than 90 days. Since Smithers & Co. appears to be the largest customer to which this company sells to on account, the owner may be hesitant to cut off the customer. Remember, though, that a customer who doesn't pay isn't really a customer. Since this customer appears to be having cash difficulties based on the slowdown in payment, the owner would need to decide to insist on immediate payment to get the account up-to-date or he or she would need to refuse to sell on account until the account is paid in full.

A second customer, Susie Landen, also needs to be investigated. Whereas her balance is not as high, the report appears to show the start of a problem. After investigation, the owner could find there is a billing dispute involving the past due amounts over 60 days. As long as the customer continues to pay for new product on time, she shouldn't get cut off while the billing dispute is investigated.

Finding the right balance for your accounts receivable policy can be critical to maintaining a good cash flow. In this business as the accounts receivable turnover indicated most customers take seven weeks to pay. You can see that by the consistent pattern of accounts with money due in the 46- to 60-day due range. If the owner of this business needs cash prior to that time to pay for inventory, he or she may need to change the accounts receivable policy.

Making changes to that policy could impact customer loyalty, so those changes shouldn't be made without consulting sales staff. For example, suppose the business owner decides he or she needs to have credit accounts paid in 30 days and implements a strict policy of cutting off customers who don't pay within that time. If the customers can open accounts with a competitor and continue to pay in 60 days, the owner could lose a lot of business.

Let's take a look at some common policy decisions that need to be made to manage the cash flow from your accounts receivable and speed up collections.

DEVELOPING ACCOUNTS RECEIVABLE POLICIES

The terms of your accounts receivable policy can be the major impediment to speeding up collections of cash from your accounts receivable. Here are some key terms that can be changed to speed up collections:

- **Credit Period:** It's obvious from the aging statement discussed earlier that this owner allows customers at least 60 days to pay. That's a liberal credit period. The owner could consider changing that to 30 days. The most conservative period would be 10 days, but changing from a liberal to a more conservative policy can drive customers away. So the decision should be made carefully after talking with your sales staff and researching the payment terms of your competitors.

- **Credit Standards:** This company's credit standards might be low, so a customer like Smithers & Co. might be given too high a credit line. The company may need to tighten its credit eligibility requirements. For example, if the company requires customers to have an income level of at least $20,000 to get a $1,000 credit, it may need to raise that to $40,000 for $1,000 in credit. Obviously, Smithers & Co. has a credit line of at least $13,500, so the owner may need to take a closer look at the credit standards that allowed Smithers & Co. to get that level of credit.

- **Collection Period:** This term can be the easiest to change to speed up collections, but it can also anger customers if you change the terms. For example, suppose you start making collection calls when a customer is more than 60 days late and decide to start the calls at 30 days. No one likes to get collection calls, but how you do the call can soften the blow. You can ask the salesperson whose commission is at risk to make the call initially to soften the approach.

- **Discounts:** One of the best tools for getting money in the door quickly is to implement a discount program. I talk about those in greater detail in Chapter 8. These help to speed collections by offering customers a discount for paying early. For example, this company could offer customers a 2 percent discount for paying in 10 days, a 1 percent discount for paying in 30 days and no discount after 30 days. This will speed up cash flow but will reduce the amount of cash the owner can expect from sales.

- **Fees and Late Payments:** Whereas discounts offer your customers a carrot for paying on time, fees and late payments hit them over the head with a stick. You can change your policy by implementing fees and late payments. For example, for any account past due you can add a collection fee of $25 for each month past due. You can also implement an interest charge for overdue accounts. For example, you can state in your credit terms that accounts accrue interest of 1.5 percent per month as soon as they become past due.

Before implementing any of these changes, it's critical to get feedback from sales managers, accounting staff, and finance staff. You must understand not only the impact on your future sales but also the impact any change in credit terms could have on your accounting staff. The change you implement could cost more staff time than you'll actually collect.

In this scenario, I reviewed the accounts receivable account of a company that appears to be having a slowdown in collections, but that's not always the problem. You may find that your customers are paying on time but your credit sales are dropping. You need to ask whether your loyal customers who were buying on account are going elsewhere. You should ask your sales staff to research credit terms of your competitors to see how your terms compare. If your terms are too conservative, you could be losing customers without even realizing why.

By looking at several years of aging schedules, you can see if your customer base is dropping and get an idea of whether you are losing customers. You may even want to call past loyal customers and find out why they are no longer shopping in your store. Aging schedules can help you find more than just a cash flow problem.

BORROWING ON RECEIVABLES

If after you've reviewed your credit policies you determine you don't want to change them, but you still need to fix a cash flow problem, you do have other options. Many companies deal with cash flow issues by implementing a receivables securitization program with their bank or other lender.

With this type of program, you actually sell your receivables to a third party in exchange for immediate cash. As receivables are collected, the amount of the loan is paid down. Often companies will maintain the responsibility of collecting from customers rather than give the servicing rights to the lender that bought the receivables. When they do that, they can negotiate a servicing fee to collect from customers. The big advantage of maintaining control of collections, however, is that the company can maintain good relations with its customers rather than having a third-party collector contact them. If a customer is a problem payer and continues to avoid paying the bill, then you probably no longer care if the customer buys from your store. At that point you may need a professional collector to get the cash from the customer.

You'll find there are two standard options for "securitizing" your receivables:

1. **Sell the receivables for less than they are worth.** In this scenario your lender will offer terms such as 92 cents for each dollar of receivables. So this equates to an 8 percent interest rate. That sounds high, but you may find that the discount for selling your receivables is the best terms you can get for a small-business loan. Compare your terms for selling your receivables with terms for other loan options and decide what's best for your company.

2. **Pay interest on the securitized receivables.** This type of loan equates to any other loan in which you secure money based on an asset. In this case the asset is your accounts receivable. For example, your bank may set up an annual interest rate of 8 percent based on the amount of money borrowed against receivables. As the customer pays, the line of credit is repaid. So although you may have an annual interest rate of 8 percent, if most of your customers pay in 30 days, you'll be borrowing money only against each customer at the rate of $\frac{1}{12}$ of 8 percent. With this type of loan, you get cash up front, making it possible to take advantage of other discounts being offered by your vendors and suppliers for early payment. I talk more about reducing your payouts in Chapter 10.

In addition to the interest you'll need to pay on the securitized receivables, you'll also likely pay up-front charges of 2 to 5 percent to set up the program with your lender. Definitely shop the market to find the best terms before signing any contracts. Of course, you should start with your regular banker, but ask other business owners you know to help you find the best deal in your area.

The biggest advantage of this type of program is that you can immediately improve your cash flow, but it does come at a price. You will need to adjust your profit expectations downward to adjust for the additional costs of securitizing your receivables. All news may not be bad. By securitizing your receivables, you may be able to increase your sales volume because you have more cash to buy inventory. You could end up actually improving your net sales numbers and your bottom line. You'd need to do a new budgeted income statement to review any projections you make based on this change to your business.

Let's take a closer look at discounts and special pricing and how they impact your bottom line in the next chapter.

TAKEAWAYS

- Although allowing customers to buy on store credit may increase your sales, you must also consider the impact this decision will have on your cash flow.

- Ask your accountant to develop a monthly aging report so that you can monitor your customer's bill paying habits and develop a collections policy that allows you to quickly deal with slow payers.

- Review your credit policies and balance them to protect your business without chasing away customers.

- You can generate cash by securitizing your accounts receivable, but be careful to assess how that will impact your bottom line.

CHAPTER 8

Discounts and Special Pricing

In This Chapter

- Understanding discounts and special pricing
- Analyzing impact of discounts
- Pros and cons of special pricing

Every business offers sales discounts to entice customers into its doors. To manage your profits and cash flow, however, you need to project the impact of any discounts or special pricing. Managing discounts and special pricing can be particularly difficult in times of an economic downturn, as we've seen since the collapse of the housing and stock market since 2007/2008. Consumers and businesses had not returned to previous spending levels at the time this book was written in 2011, and there were few signs that this would change anytime soon.

To get customers, most companies were instituting deep discounts to move inventory off their shelves. Even a tried-and-true company like Campbell's Soup warned in 2011 that it had to lower its projected revenue and earnings because of deep discounting.

As you prepare your budget at the beginning of the year, you should estimate what percentage of your product will be sold at a discount. Depending on demand during the year, you may find that you need to discount your products even more to sell them. Tracking your sales discounts through the year will help you monitor your bottom line and your potential of meeting your profit goals.

In this chapter, I take a closer look at sales discounts and how to use a budgeted income statement to monitor their impact throughout the sales year. Then I focus on special pricing and how that could help or hurt your profit expectations.

DISCOUNT OR SPECIAL PRICE

Discounts and special pricing serve a very different role in business. A discount is advertised publicly by media advertising, direct mail, or signs in the store. Special pricing usually is done more privately with negotiations between your company and a potential large customer. While a discount may be a percentage or dollar amount off one particular purchase, a special price agreement will likely be a long-term contract to offer reduced pricing based on a certain volume of business.

Whether it's wise to make this special pricing deal will depend on how that lowered price will impact your business. It can be a win/win for both you and your customer or it can be a disaster to your bottom line. You need to calculate the variables and prepare a projected budgeted income statement to assess the deal's impact on your bottom line before agreeing to any special pricing deal. I show you how to do that later in the chapter, but first let's take a closer look at how discounts impact your bottom line.

TRACKING THE IMPACT OF DISCOUNTS ON YOUR BOTTOM LINE

You've likely offered your customers a discount on some product or service to get them in the door. For example, many car repair businesses regularly send out flyers offering services at discounted rates, hoping to get customers in the door so that they can then sell the customer on additional full-price services. At the very least, these businesses use discounts to introduce their services to new customers, hoping they will return for additional services.

The key question you must ask yourself before offering a discount, however, is do you know how that discount will ultimately impact your bottom line. When you prepare your initial budget, you should review your discount policies from the previous year, estimate how much your business lost in revenue to discounts, and estimate what you think the impact will be on your business in the next year.

You can easily view the impact of discounts by asking your accountant for an internal report that details the accounts that impact the sales figure shown on your income statement. For example, here's the most common accounts that impact the net sales figures:

Gross Sales	$50,000
Less: Discounts	($5,000)
Less: Returns	($2,000)
Less: Allowances	($2,000)
Net Sales	$41,000

On an external income statement you'll see only the Net Sales figure, but for profit planning purposes it's important to ask your accountant for this additional detail. In this particular example, you can see that the company regularly offers its sales at a 10 percent discount. It can expect about 4 percent of its sales to be returned and another 4 percent of its products to be taken based on allowances. These allowances are likely gift cards that were redeemed.

When this company prepares its budgeted income statement, it needs to consider these factors when determining net sales for the next year. The assumptions regarding percentages for discounts, returns, and allowances should be recorded. When the budgeted income statement variables are prepared, red flags should alert the readers of the statements through the year that compare budgeted numbers with actual numbers. Whenever the discounts, returns or allowances exceed their estimated percentages, the owner should get an indication with a red flag. Pick a particular icon to indicate a red flag. I use arrows as red flags for this example.

Your monthly budgeted versus actual sales report could look something like this:

	Budget	Actual	Flag
Gross Sales	$50,000	$48,000	↓
Less: Discounts	$5,000	$4,800	↓
Less: Returns	$2,000	$2,000	
Less: Allowances	$2,000	$2,000	
Net Sales	$41,000	$39,200	↓

As you can see from this report, the business owner can quickly find the line items that are lower than expected. A downward pointing arrow indicates a number below what was budgeted. An upward pointing arrow would be used for numbers above expectations. A difference of $2,000 in sales for one month may not be a critical difference for this business. The relative importance of a red flag to your business is your call.

By reviewing these key line items on a detailed budgeted income statement for sales, you can quickly pick up problems and look for solutions that can be implemented in the next month rather than let the problems fester throughout the year and result in a major reduction in anticipated profits.

SPECIAL PRICING: PRO OR CON?

Special pricing can be a help or a hindrance to your profit goals. Before agreeing to a special pricing deal, you need to determine how that deal will impact your bottom line by preparing a projected income statement that includes the key line items to be impacted by that special deal.

For example, suppose a customer comes to you and says that he will guarantee to purchase 500 widgets for $18 on a monthly basis. Your normal selling price for widgets is $20. Is that a good deal? At first glance you might think, Why would I accept the lower price even for that volume of sales? Looking at only these numbers it appears to be a loss of $1,000 in sales. But these are not the only line items that could be impacted by this deal.

You may have an agreement with your supplier that reduces the price for widgets based on volume purchasing. After reviewing the contract, you find that your price for widgets is $15 when you buy 5,000 per year, but it goes down to $14 when you buy 10,000 per year. If you projected to sell 500 widgets per month or 6,000 per year and this deal will enable you to take advantage of the lower price for all your widgets, you'd need to do a new projected budgeted income statement to see what the real impact would be on your bottom line.

Let's take a look at how this special pricing deal will impact the bottom line:

	Original Budget	Projected Special Pricing Budget
Net Sales	$120,000	$228,000
Cost of Goods Sold	$90,000	$168,000
Gross Profit	$30,000	$60,000

In preparing these numbers, I calculated the original budget based on 6,000 units sold at $20, for a total net sales of $120,000. I calculated the cost of goods sold based on a price of $15 (15 × 6,000) for a total of $90,000. When calculating the projected special pricing budget, I calculated the first 6,000 units to be sold at $20 (20 × 6,000) and the special deal 6,000 units to be sold at $18 (18 × 6,000); I then totaled these calculations to get a net sales number of $228,000. On the special budget, I calculated all 12,000 units at the volume pricing of $14 for a cost of goods sold total of $168,000. With this deal, the business owner will be able to buy all units, not just the units for the special pricing deal, at the lowered cost of goods sold price. That helped improve the owner's bottom line for the originally projected sales.

Not only would this deal increase the gross profit on this company's projected sales for the year, but the increased volume and lower pricing for cost of goods sold will double the gross profit. In this case the owner does not anticipate the special deal will involve any extra staff time or other extra costs, but if you do think other line items on your budget will be impacted by a special pricing deal you're considering, it's important to show those impacts on the projected special budget as well. For example, if you think the special pricing deal will result in additional staff time or other expenses, you would want to include the expense section in the projected budget and show the impacts to the bottom line.

Whenever your salespeople come to you with a special pricing deal, it's critical that you consider all variables that will be impacted by the deal and project a new budget based on these new variables. As long as you will see an improvement in the bottom line, then the deal makes sense for your business.

Now let's take a closer look at how you can get a handle on costs, especially if you're operating a manufacturing company.

TAKEAWAYS

- Discounts lower profits, but they can be a necessary evil to drive customers to your business. It's important to track your discounts throughout the year and be certain they are staying within budget. If not, investigate and adjust your sales strategy or lower your profit expectations.

- Special pricing can be both the boon and the bane for your business. Prepare a projected income statement that shows the key line items to be impacted by the deal to determine whether the special pricing will help or hurt your business.

CHAPTER 9

Getting a Handle on Manufacturing Costs

In This Chapter

- Understanding costs in a manufacturing environment
- Developing reports to monitor costs
- Exploring the difference between fixed and variable costs
- Determining benefits of special pricing deals

Getting a handle on cost of goods sold in a manufacturing business can be much more difficult than in a nonmanufacturing environment. In Chapter 6, I introduced you to concepts of how to value inventory. If you own a manufacturing company, you don't purchase goods. Instead you purchase raw materials and incur other costs to get to the point of having finished goods for sale. So you need to do a lot more calculations to find out your cost of goods sold for your income statement and to determine the value of that inventory on the balance sheet.

In this chapter, I introduce you to the key variables you must manage to get a handle on costs in a manufacturing environment. I show you how to develop an internal report that will allow you to keep an eye on these variables throughout the year and make changes midterm if your cost of goods sold will be higher or lower than budgeted. Then I explore the difference with fixed and variable costs and how you use that difference to make decisions to improve your bottom line.

DETERMINING COST OF GOODS SOLD IN MANUFACTURING

If you own a manufacturing business, you know that there's a lot more involved than buying goods to sell to customers. You may not be aware of all the moving parts involved in getting to that cost of goods manufactured number. Here are the key elements:

- **Raw Materials:** These are the goods you must buy in order to make your product. When calculating cost of goods sold, you'll be considering new purchases of raw materials during the current accounting period as well as raw materials you have on hand from the previous accounting period. This can be calculated on a monthly, quarterly, or yearly basis.

- **Direct Labor:** These costs include the wages you pay to workers to make your finished goods. Direct labor includes only those workers who are involved in making the product. The wages for all other workers are calculated as part of manufacturing overhead.

- **Manufacturing Overhead:** These costs include everything you spend to make your product that is not directly calculated into the costs of each finished product. For example, you'll have indirect materials, such as screws, nails, and other items that you may not want to take the time to count and cost each time you make a product. You more likely purchase these types of items in bulk for many different products you manufacture. You'll also have indirect labor. These will be people you pay who support the manufacturing process, such as your purchasing staff, who do not work directly on manufacturing products. Indirect labor also will include janitors, night security guards, engineers, and so on. Other costs include depreciation of your factory equipment and building, insurance, utilities, and possibly machine rental.

- **Work in Progress Inventory:** This will include any inventory that was not yet completed and ready for sale during the previous accounting period.

You, your manufacturing manager, and your accountant should review the costs that go into your manufacturing process and determine what should be a line item for direct costs and what should be calculated as part of your manufacturing overhead. When you've figured all that out, you can develop an internal report called a "Schedule of Cost of Goods Manufactured" that looks something like this:

	Budget	Actual	Flag
Direct Materials			
Beginning raw materials inventory	$100,000		
Add: Purchases of raw materials	$150,000		
Raw materials available for use	$160,000		
Deduct: Ending raw materials inventory	$7,500		
Raw materials used in production	$152,500		
Direct Labor	$275,000		
Manufacturing Overhead			
Indirect materials	$5,000		
Indirect labor	$75,000		
Utilities: factory	$50,000		
Insurance: factory	$20,000		
Depreciation: factory	$80,000		
Property taxes: factory	$7,000		
Total overhead costs	$237,000		
Total manufacturing costs	$512,000		
Add: Beginning work in progress inventory	$50,000		
Deduct: Ending work in progress inventory	$40,000		
Cost of goods manufactured	$522,000		

You can use this report to track your manufacturing costs through-out the year. As with the income statement, you likely want to ask your accountant to prepare both a year-to-date report and a monthly report. Your monthly report should be developed based on historical records of your manufacturing activity. As you review manufacturing activity in prior years, you'll likely find some months, such as those getting ready to fill orders before a holiday season, have higher level of production than other months. By monitoring these numbers on a month-to-month basis, you can quickly see whether your manu-facturing team is staying on budget. If not, investigate the items that get flagged so that you can deal with any problems as quickly as pos-sible to reduce the potential for a negative impact on your company's bottom line.

INVENTORY VALUE IN A MANUFACTURING ENVIRONMENT

Calculations for cost of goods sold are not the only differences you'll see in financial reports for a manufacturing company. The value of inventory also will be impacted. On an external report you may find only one number on the balance sheet for inventory value, but internally you need more detail to understand the value of your inventory asset if you're operating a manufacturing business. That value is based on three variables:

1. **Raw Materials:** The value of the materials you have on hand for future manufacturing

2. **Work in Progress:** The value of the partially completed products on hand

3. **Finished Goods:** The value of goods available for sale, but not yet sold

You do want to get a monthly report that shows these three values and watch for trends in the values. If the raw materials value trends upward, it could mean one of two things: The costs of these materials are going up or you're maintaining a higher level of inventory than you need. You need to investigate the reason for the upward trend and make adjustments in your purchasing decisions to minimize the impact. Since buying raw materials can be a drain on cash, you can improve your company's cash position by getting a handle on raw materials costs.

The key to managing inventory costs in a manufacturing environment is finding the right balance between having raw materials on hand to avoid slowing down the manufacturing process, while at the same time minimizing your costs of buying and carrying that inventory. Work with your manufacturing and financing staff to determine that proper balance.

The companies that master that art determine a "just in time" inventory process that calculates the right time to order new raw materials to be sure they will be on hand when needed by manufacturing, but not too early so that your company incurs increased storage and purchasing costs. That right answer differs company by company. If you miscalculate the right time to order new raw materials and you don't have them on hand when needed by manufacturing, it means your entire line could be closed down. So finding that optimal reorder point can be crucial to managing both costs of goods sold and inventory value.

EXPLORING FIXED VERSUS VARIABLE COSTS

All types of businesses have fixed and variable costs. The fixed costs are costs that you must pay just to open the doors of your business. The variable costs are those that vary based on the volume of your business. Getting control over your variable costs can go a long way to improving your bottom line.

In a retail business your primary variable cost is the cost of goods sold. You decide how many goods you will buy depending on your estimates of customer demand. You also can control your costs by negotiating better deals with your suppliers and vendors. Other variable costs include your staffing levels and the commissions you pay your salespeople. If your business is slower than expected, you can reduce staff levels or reduce your future purchases. The primary fixed cost is the rental on retail and office space that you must pay even if you have no customers walking in the door. You also have fixed costs in the furniture and fixtures in your stores, but you're not likely laying out cash on a monthly basis so that won't impact your ability to keep the business operating. If you have rented the furniture or fixtures, you may be able to return some of them to reduce monthly costs. In this scenario your furniture or fixtures could be a variable cost.

If you own a service business, your primary variable costs are supplies, travel, and clerical staff. You may be able to reduce professional staff, but that will also likely reduce your chances of bringing in new business; this generally means that a service business will reduce staff levels more slowly than a retail business. Your primary fixed cost is the rent you pay for your offices. If you've rented equipment and furniture that, too, could be a variable cost, depending on whether you can return the furniture and reduce your monthly expenses.

Manufacturing businesses have a much heavier load to carry when it comes to fixed costs. They must pay for the operation of plant facilities, as well as the operation of office facilities. These facilities likely devour cash every month, even if no products are moving out the door. Maintenance must be done on the facilities to keep the machinery and other equipment in working order so that when business picks up they will still be in good shape.

Variable costs for a manufacturing facility are primarily in the costs of direct materials and direct labor. When business is booming, the company increases the purchase of raw materials. If the business faces a slowdown, it can quickly adjust its ordering to reduce the cash outlay for raw materials. The same is true for direct labor. When business is slow, the manufacturing company can cut labor hours or lay people off until business picks up.

When you're operating a manufacturing business, it's critical to understand which costs are fixed and which are variable. To make matters even more confusing, some costs are mixed costs—they vary depending on manufacturing level. For example, maintenance costs may go up when the machinery is running more frequently.

Work with your accounting team to determine these differences so that you can develop a monthly fixed cost for operating your facility as well as a variable cost per unit for manufacturing new product. These numbers will help you to make better pricing decisions. For example, you may decide after doing market research that by reducing your price you could sell more products. You could improve your bottom line because you'll be spreading the fixed cost among a greater number of product sales. Even though you may decide to offer your products at a lower price, the higher volume could result in a higher net profit.

To make this decision, you first need to calculate your profit and loss statement for your expected business level at the current price. For example, I start with the assumption that you calculate your monthly fixed costs as $20,000 for manufacturing your products. You must spend that money each month even if you manufacture nothing. Then you calculate your direct labor cost per unit is $3.00 and your direct materials cost per unit is $2.50. Both of these costs are variable costs. You sell your product for $20, and you estimate that you will sell 4,000 units per month. What's your monthly gross profit? Here's how it would be calculated:

Sales	$80,000 (4,000 × 20)
Cost of Goods Manufactured	
Direct labor	12,000 (4,000 × 3)
Direct materials	10,000 (4,000 × 2.50)
Manufacturing overhead	$20,000
Gross Profit	$38,000

For this business to earn a profit, the expenses would need to be lower than $38,000. You can then use this information to develop a budgeted monthly income statement that will help monitor your success at meeting your net income goals for the year.

	Budget	**Actual**	**Flag**
Sales	$80,000		
Cost of Goods Manufactured			
Direct labor	12,000		
Direct materials	10,000		
Manufacturing overhead	$20,000		
Gross Profit	$38,000		
Expenses	$22,000		
Net Income	$16,000		

In this example I do not detail the line items for expenses. You can decide how much detail you want to show in the expenses section of the budgeted income statement. You don't need to show every line item, but it's good to show any line items that can vary significantly throughout the year so that you can keep a close eye on expenses.

SPECIAL PRICING DEALS AND MANUFACTURING

Now let's suppose this business owner was offered a special pricing deal by a major customer who agreed to buy 4,000 units per month at $18. Would it be worth it for the owner to consider this special pricing deal at a discount of $2 per unit?

First, the business owner would need to determine whether the current facilities could handle that increased level of production. If so, will it mean a lot of overtime or additional maintenance costs? To keep things simple, I assume that the added production will impact only the variable costs for direct labor and materials. The market was slow and there was plenty of capacity left within the existing facilities. The expense line items would not be impacted. Here's a projected income statement for the new business:

	Budgeted	Special Pricing Deal	Total
Sales	$80,000	$72,000	$152,000
Cost of Goods Manufactured			
Direct labor	12,000	$12,000	$24,000
Direct materials	10,000	$10,000	$20,000
Manufacturing overhead	$20,000		$20,000
Gross Profit	$38,000		$88,000
Expenses	$20,000		$20,000
Net Income	$18,000		$68,000

You can see that even though the two variable costs double, the bottom line more than tripled, because with this deal the fixed costs are allocated to more completed units. Let's take a closer look at what happened to the per unit cost.

When the company was manufacturing just 4,000 units, the cost of goods manufactured was $12,000 plus $10,000 plus $20,000 for a total of $42,000 or $10.50 ($42,000/4,000) per unit and the product was sold for $20.00. With the special pricing deal, 8,000 units were produced for a cost of goods manufactured that totaled $64,000 (24,000 + 20,000 + 20,000). That's comes out to a cost of just $8 ($64,000/8,000) per unit. The business owner was able to produce even the budgeted inventory at the reduced rate of $8 and sell them for an additional $2.50 profit ($10.50 original per unit cost minus $8 new per unit cost with increased production). In a manufacturing environment special pricing deals can be more complicated to calculate. Nevertheless as long as the capacity is there, these deals will usually end up being a benefit to the company even at a reduced price because the company is making more efficient use of existing facilities.

CALCULATING THE IMPACT OF LOWER PRICES

You can do a similar analysis if you decide to lower your prices in an attempt to get more business in the door. Let's suppose you decide to lower your prices by $2 per unit to $18. After a market analysis you think this price change could increase your sales by 2,000 per month. Would that improve your bottom line? Here's how to do that calculation using the same variables as discussed in the previous section: $20,000 fixed costs, $3 direct labor per unit, and $2.50 direct materials per unit.

Sales	$108,000 (6,000 × 18)
Cost of Goods Manufactured	
Direct labor	18,000 (6,000 × 3)
Direct materials	15,000 (6,000 × 2.50)
Manufacturing overhead	$20,000
Gross Profit	$55,000

As you can see with this scenario, as long as you can increase your sales by 2,000 units if you lower your price $2 to $18, then it would be worth making the decision to lower the price. The gross profit, even after lowering the price by $2 to $18, is $17,000 higher than the $38,000 calculated previously, with just 4,000 units sold at $20.

Now that we've looked at the costs, let's see how you can reduce cash payouts with proper management of bill payment in the next chapter.

TAKEAWAYS

- Calculating costs of goods sold in a manufacturing environment involves more than just purchases of raw materials to make your product. You need to develop a good understanding of the other costs involved: direct labor, direct materials, and manufacturing overhead.

- If you're operating a manufacturing company, your inventory value is not just the finished goods ready for sale. You must also include raw materials on hand and work in progress inventory.

- Get a handle on your company's fixed and variable costs. The fixed costs you must pay out each month. Getting a better handle on the variable costs can go a long way to improving your bottom line.

CHAPTER 10

Reducing Bill Payouts

In This Chapter

- Quickly paying your bills
- Taking advantage of discounts
- Managing your bill payments

Your company's ability to get the products or raw materials when you need them depends greatly on your company's bill-paying history. If you get the reputation for paying your bills late, you could lose your ability to buy on credit. Even if you can still get credit, your interest rates on that credit will probably soar. So it's always important to pay those bills on time or to work out a deal with your suppliers, vendors, and bankers.

Paying those bills just in time on the day they are due may not be your best option, however. Often companies offer discounts for paying earlier than the final due date. You may find you can actually improve your bottom line by taking advantage of these discounts.

In this chapter, I first show you how to calculate the accounts payable ratio and how it can impact your business decisions. Then I review how using discounts can actually improve your profits. Finally, if the worst-case scenario strikes, I discuss strategies you can employ to slow down your bill payment during a cash crunch.

YOUR BILL-PAYING TURNOVER

Let's start by testing your company's bill-paying record. You can do that using the accounts payable turnover ratio and then determining the number of days it takes your company to pay a bill. The accounts payable turnover ratio measures how quickly a company pays its bills.

You calculate this ratio by dividing the cost of goods sold (shown on the income statement) by the average accounts payable (shown on the balance sheet). This is a two-step process:

1. **Find the average accounts payable.** Add the accounts payable total from the previous year and the accounts payable total from the current year; divide the number by 2.

2. **Calculate the accounts payable turnover.** Divide the cost of goods sold number by the average accounts payable number.

To show you how this works, let's assume the accounts payable number shown on the balance sheet in 2010 was $82,000 and the accounts payable number shown on the balance sheet in 2011 was $102.500. The cost of goods sold number on the income statement was $825,000. Here's the calculation:

$$1. \ \frac{(\$82,000 + \$102,500)}{2} = \$92,250$$

$$2. \ \frac{\$825,000}{\$92,250} = 8.9$$

This company turns over its accounts payable 8.9 times a year. The higher the accounts payable turnover ratio, the shorter the time between purchase of goods and payment for those goods. If the turnover ratio is a low number, then it could be an indication that a company is having a hard time paying its bills. What's a good number? That will vary greatly by industry. The key is to watch the trend if the number is gradually going up; it's a good sign. It means the company is paying bills in a shorter period of time. If the number is gradually going down, it means the company may be having more difficulty paying its bills.

So how does this calculation translate into how many days it takes your company to pay a bill on average? You need to calculate the number of days in the accounts payable ratio. If you calculate this ratio for a number of years and see that it's taking longer and longer to pay bills it could be a sign of a cash flow problem.

Here's the formula for calculating the number of days in an accounts payable ratio:

$$\text{Days in Accounts Payable} = \frac{\text{Average Accounts Payable}}{\text{Cost of Goods Sold}} \times 360 \text{ Days}$$

In accounting, the number for a year is usually 360 days so that the calculation can be based on a 30-day month. Here's the calculation using the same numbers shown in the previous example to calculate the number of days in accounts payable:

$$\frac{\$92{,}250}{\$825{,}000} \times 360 = 40.25 \text{ Days}$$

So this company takes, on average, 40 days to pay its bills. Is it experiencing a cash flow problem? You can quickly tell that by calculating two other ratios: average sales credit period shown to you in Chapter 7 and the number of days to sell inventory. As long as the company is selling its inventory more frequently than it pays its bills, there's likely no cash flow problem. But you also need to look at how quickly customers are paying their bills. If customer payments are taking longer than the number of days listed in accounts payable, you could face a cash flow problem.

What's the best number for your company? That depends on a lot of factors, such as how quickly you can sell your goods and how quickly you collect from your customers. You can also talk with your local Chamber of Commerce to see if it tracks any of these ratios so that you can compare your figures with those of other companies. Your industry association may be another good source for ratios within your industry.

EVALUATING BILL PAYMENT DISCOUNT OFFERS

Just as you want to bring in cash more quickly by offering discounts, so do your vendors and suppliers. They will likely offer you discounts to pay your bills early. You need to determine whether this discount is worth it to your company.

You can often find terms for discounts at the top of a bill. For example, you may see at the top of your bill the terms "2/10 net 30" or "3/10 net 60." If you see "2/10 net 30," it means that you can take a 2 percent discount if you pay the bill in 10 days or you can pay the full bill in 30 days. If you see "3/10 net 60," then it means that you can take a 3 percent discount if you pay the bill in 10 days or you can pay the bill in full in 60 days.

Taking advantage of these discounts can save you a lot of money over the year, but if you just don't have the cash on hand to pay the bill early you have to determine whether it's worth it to use your company's credit line to take advantage of this discount. You do this by comparing the interest saved by taking the discount with the interest you must pay to use your credit line if you pay the bills early.

You can evaluate the value of discounts by calculating the annual interest rate of the discount. The formula for calculating the annual interest rate is:

$$\frac{\% \ Discount}{100\% \ Discount} \times \frac{360}{Number \ of \ Days \ Paid \ Early} = Annual \ Interest \ Rate$$

Note: Formula should be shown as:

$$\frac{\% \ Discount}{100 - \% \ Discount} \times \frac{360}{Number \ of \ Days \ Paid \ Early} = Annual \ Interest \ Rate$$

The key difference is "$100 - \%$ Discount" not "100% Discount."

Evaluating 2/10 Net 30

Let's calculate the annual interest rate for the terms of 2/10 net 30:

$$\frac{2}{98(100 - 2)} \times \frac{360}{20 \ (Number \ of \ Days \ Paid \ Early)} = 36.73\%$$

Since that annual interest rate is considerably higher than the interest rate the company is likely to pay if it needs to use its credit line to meet cash flow demands, it makes a lot of sense to pay the bill early as long as the credit line is available.

Let's assume you purchased $100,000 in inventory and can pay based on the terms of 2/10 net 30. If you take advantage of that 2 percent discount, you can take $2,000 off the bill and pay only $98,000. Even if you must borrow the $98,000 for 20 days until the inventory has been sold, you likely will pay less than that in interest on your credit line. Let's assume you have a credit line you can tap at 14 percent. Interest at 14 percent for 20 days on $98,000 would cost you $751.80 in interest [(98,000 × 0.14)/365 = $37.59 per day]. That means you'll save $1,248.20 by paying early, even though you have to pay interest. That savings gets added directly to your net profit.

Evaluating 3/10 Net 60

What about 3/10 net 60? Is it still worth it paying 50 days early? Let's calculate the annual interest rate for the terms 3/10 net 30 on a $100,000 bill:

$$\frac{3}{97(100 - 3)} \times \frac{360}{50 \text{ (Number of Days Paid Early)}} = 22.27\%$$

You can see that the interest rate is considerably lower for these terms. The annual interest rate with these terms is 22.27 percent. It's still likely higher than the interest rate you will need to pay using your credit line. In this scenario the cost of interest on $98,000 for 50 days at 14 percent ($37.59) would be $1,879.50 in interest. There is only a small savings of $120.50. That can add up over the year. You can increase this savings by paying down the credit line as the inventory sells rather than wait the full 50 days to pay off the credit line.

You can see from these calculations that it's often a cash savings to take advantage of discount terms. Organize your accounts payable to track and use discount terms. Calculate the annual interest rate for these discounts and instruct your accounts payable staff person when to take advantage of the discount and pay the bill early.

DELAYING BILL PAYMENT

Getting credit can sometimes be difficult for a small business, especially after a major downturn like the one we began experiencing in 2008. For a while small businesses were not able to get a credit line and, in many cases, those that had credit lines lost them or had their allowable credit lines decreased. When that happens, your company can face a cash crunch and may have to decide to slow down paying the bills.

Don't make that decision on your own without consulting your suppliers and vendors. If you've been a good customer for many years, you likely will be able to work out some type of trade financing. Trade financing essentially allows you to delay cash payment based on a set of terms you work out with your vendor or supplier that may include interest or fees for late payment. Whatever the terms, trade financing enables you to stay in business through slow times and still have products on the shelves to satisfy customer demand. When you can't get credit through a lender, this may be your only option to stay in business.

You do need to adjust your budgeted income statement to reflect the higher costs of goods sold and determine whether you can still make a profit. You'll likely need to lower your profit projections.

Some businesses won't even try to work out terms with their suppliers. They'll just start paying late until they get cut off completely. This practice is known as stretching accounts payable or riding the trade.

You do get an advantage for a short time to "ride the trade," but ultimately you likely will face losing the supplier or vendor and wrecking the reputation of your business. When the economy turns around, you'll find it difficult to get credit from both vendors and lenders. If you want to stay in business when the economy recovers after a recession, work with your vendors, suppliers, and bankers throughout the bad times. Don't just take it upon yourself to decide your business' payment terms.

TAKEAWAYS

- Calculate your accounts payable ratio and compare that with how quickly you're turning over your inventory and how quickly your customers are paying the bills. If you need to pay your bills before you bring in the cash from sales, you likely will face a cash crunch.

- You can improve your bottom line by taking advantage of discounts. Calculate the annual interest rate for the discount and compare it with the interest you must pay on your credit line. Pay the bill early and take advantage of the discount if it will save you more money than you would need to pay in interest on your credit line.

- If you face a cash shortfall, don't decide on your own how to deal with the problem. Work closely with your vendors and suppliers to avoid being cut off or ruining your company's reputation.

Conclusion

Using Financial Statements
for Decision Making

Throughout this book I introduce you to ways you can use financial statements to improve your decision making. External reports give information to your bankers, vendors, and suppliers, as well as to people inside the company who you do not want to have full access to the financial details.

Internal financial reports are the ones you truly need to manage your finances and make intelligent decisions for your business. Sit down with your accountant and develop customized internal reports that will help you quickly identify any problem areas. There are no rules for internal reports, so it's up to you to decide the information you want to track periodically, whether it's weekly, monthly, quarterly, or yearly.

Initially it may take some time to design these customized reports, but, once designed, the computerized accounting system can generate them automatically in seconds. That initial time you spend designing the reports to your company's specific needs will be well worth the effort for many years to come. As your company grows, you may find you need detail about other key bits of information. The report designs are not written in stone; you can tweak them at any time to help you make more informed decisions to run your company.

Take advantage of both types of financial reports to gauge how well you are doing by researching industry information through BizStats (www.bizstats.com). You may also be able to get average ratios through your local Chamber of Commerce or through your industry associations.

With the statistics in hand and by calculating the ratios for your business as I show you in this book, you should be able to quickly identify problem areas. Start working on ways to improve your results, which ultimately will mean a more profitable bottom line. Improvements will be found not only by increasing revenue; getting a handle on costs and expenses can sometimes be even more rewarding for your bottom line.

About the Author

Lita Epstein is a seasoned financial writer with more than 25 books on the market. She earned her MBA at Emory University's Goizueta Business School. While completing her degree at Emory, she was hired as a graduate assistant to run the accounting laboratory for MBA and executive MBA candidates.

Upon graduating from Emory, Lita raised millions of dollars for The Carter Center to support the international peace efforts and other international projects of former President Jimmy Carter. She then managed finances for a small nonprofit before taking a job as a financial manager for The Emory Clinics. At the clinics she managed the finances for five departments under Facilities Management—Guest Services, Mail Room, Maintenance, Material Services, and Transportation.

Now she enjoys helping individuals and companies develop good financial, investing, and tax-planning skills. Her books include *Reading Financial Reports For Dummies, Bookkeeping For Dummies, Bookkeeping Workbook For Dummies, Streetwise Crash Course MBA,* and *Surviving a Layoff: A Week-by-Week Guide to Getting Your Life Back Together.*

She also writes periodically for AOL's online blogs, including "AOL Real Estate" and "AOL Daily Finance."

Index

cost of goods or services
   sold (*continued*)
   vs. expenses, 61
   tracking cost of on income
      statements, 59–60
cost of goods sold accounts, 21
cost of goods sold in manufacturing
   described, 60, 143–145
   fixed *vs.* variable costs, ·
      147–149, 152
   lower prices, calculating impact
      of, 151–152
   Schedule of Cost of Goods
      Manufactured report, 144–145
costs, defined, 6
credit, obtaining, 43–47
   See also accounts receivable
credit card payable accounts, 19
creditors, as financial report
   readers, 7
credit period, 127
credit policies, 127–129, 131
credits and debits, 12–14
credit standards, 128
current assets, 32–40
current assets accounts, 16
current cash debt coverage ratio,
   88–89
urrent liabilities, 40–41
rrent liabilities accounts, 18–19
rent portion of long-term
   debt, 41
nt ratio, 43–44
ier accounts, monitoring, 123

nce sheets, 29–30
me statements, 52–53
redits, 12–14

debt, financing activities and, 84
   See also borrowing; liabilities
debt payoff, 84–85
debt-to-equity ratio, 45–47
decision making
   in budget development, 96
   using financial statements for,
      163–164
depreciation
   buildings, 17, 38
   cash flow depreciation expenses,
      79–80
   equipment, 17
   expenses on income statements, 62
   leasehold improvements, 17
depreciation and amortization
   expense accounts, 22
direct labor, 144
direct method format, statement of
   cash flows, 75–76, 79
discontinued operations, 85
discounts
   in accounts receivable, 128
   annual interest rates of,
      calculating, 157–159, 161
   bill payment discount offers,
      157–160
   bottom line, impact on,
      136–138, 140
   defined, 136
   price structures, changing,
      60–61
   sales discounts and revenue
      recognition, 57–58
   sales discounts as revenue
      account, 20–21
   vs. special pricing, 136
   types of, 58
   volume discounts, 58